ALIVE & WELL

Discovering

God's Presence

in the Midst of

Everyday Life

Diane S. Knight

ALIVE & WELL
Discovering God's Presence in the Midst of Everyday Life

Word Alive Press
131 Cordite Road, Winnipeg, MB R3W 1S1
www.wordalivepress.ca

Mixed Sources
Cert no. SW-COC-001271
© 1996 FSC

Library and Archives Canada Cataloguing in Publication

Knight, Diane S., 1964-
   Alive and well : discovering God's presence in the midst of everyday life / Diane S. Knight.

ISBN 978-1-77069-133-9

   1. Spiritual life--Christianity. 2. Christian life. I. Title.

BV4501.3.K55 2010   248.4   C2010-907260-X

This book is dedicated to my special son, Justin, who had a love for others and a joyful approach to life. He interacted with God in simple, joyful ways. His life and death have taught me much about God.

Acknowledgements

In writing a book that focuses on the lessons God has been teaching me about Himself, through the life and passing of my special needs son, I have discovered that such an enormous undertaking could not be approached without the prayers and assistance of many supportive friends. Of particular note, my husband Dan has stood beside me every step of the way, providing all the help and encouragement I needed to complete this very challenging task.

I want to thank those who have prayed for me throughout this process. It was God who spoke through people and circumstances to convince me to write this book, and it was He who enabled me to write it. I must also thank the five people who helped me with the enormous job of editing this book—Kathy, Kathy, Jim, Viola, and Sue. Their hours of hard work and dedication are what made the final product possible. I am very grateful for Graham Punter, who created the drawing for the final chapter. A special thank you needs to be given to Edna Massimilla, author of *Heaven's Very Special Child and the Family*, who graciously allowed me to use her poem "Heaven's Very Special Child" and to Katrina Kenison, who allowed me to quote from her book, *Mitten Strings for God: Reflections for Mothers in a Hurry*. Finally, I would like to thank Jen Jandavs-Hedlin of Word Alive Press, whose friendly and efficient assistance made the publication process straightforward, and to Evan Braun of Word Alive Press, who did the final editing.

It is my hope and prayer that, by reading this book, you will sense the heart of God and His desire to be all He can be in your day-to-day life.

Table of Contents

CHAPTER ONE
God Prepares Us

Bel bows down; Nebo stoops;
Their idols are on beasts and livestock;
These things you carry are borne
as burdens on weary beasts.
They stoop; they bow down together;
they cannot save the burden,
but themselves go into captivity.

          —ISAIAH 46:1–2 (ESV)

The earth is the Lord's and the fullness thereof,
the world and those who dwell therein.

          —PSALM 24:1 (ESV)

1

Teaching in small town Alberta brought many changes and challenges into my life as I began my career in my early twenties. Discipline was a test for me, as I was somewhat shy and no taller than my Grade Five students. Still, I enjoyed the children immensely and especially loved to read their stories of calving, crop harvesting, and 4H club. All this was so new to me, for I had grown up in a small town in the mountains of British Columbia and attended university in the big city.

That year my new friend, who taught in the resource room, told me she would be taking her maternity leave. She informed our principal that I was a special education teacher with the necessary qualifications to assume her position in the fall. What a thrill it was to be assigned to my first special needs classroom, with a supportive aide and eight good-natured students. I loved the intimate atmosphere that our little group allowed as we worked together like a family.

On the home front, my husband and I were trying to start our own family. My first pregnancy had ended suddenly and sadly in miscarriage during my third year of teaching. I didn't fully grieve the loss of that first child until years later, when I realized that I needed to mourn and name my child Michael. Miscarriage is a hidden death that, sadly, we often don't know how to grieve. Someday, Michael and I will meet in heaven.

Now I was pregnant again. Over and over during my pregnancy, many people said to me, "I hope you have a healthy baby!"

I began to question this statement and thought to myself, *What if I don't have a normal, healthy baby?*

Easter Sunday came and several members of our extended family were in our living room discussing the upcoming arrival of our baby. I sat quietly, listening to the discussion. Some were predicting I would have a baby boy, while others seemed sure it was a girl. All seemed to have a reason for their prediction.

Then the discussion moved to their desire for us to have a healthy baby. Again I wondered at this statement. Truthfully, shouldn't we want to celebrate the arrival of *any* child, healthy or not?

Maybe those thoughts were there because I was a special education teacher. Still, does every special education teacher who is pregnant expect the possibility of not having a healthy baby? "I just want a baby with blue eyes!" I said to myself with conviction.

God heard my little prayer that day and honored my request. He prepared me for the birth of our very special second child. He prepared my heart and caused me to question the expectation that our child would be born healthy. God had a purpose for our lives—one that He was just beginning to unfold. *"Declaring the end from the beginning and from ancient times things not yet done, saying, 'My counsel shall stand, and I will accomplish all my purpose'"* (Isaiah 46:10, ESV).

I hadn't met the living God at that point in my life. I had heard of Him at church, but I didn't know Him personally. But God knew me, and because of His tremendous love He was preparing me for what was to come.

God is a living God; He is alive today and has been for eternity. As it states at the very beginning of the Bible, in Genesis 1:1–2, *"In the beginning God created the heavens and the earth. Now the earth was formless and empty, darkness was over the surface of the deep, and the Spirit of God was hovering over the waters"* (NIV). These verses speak of God the Father and the Holy Spirit being alive before the earth was formed. In the first verses of the Book of John, it speaks of where Jesus (the Word) was at that same time: *"In the beginning was the Word, and the Word was with God, and the Word was God. He was with God in the beginning. Through him all things were made; without him nothing was made that has been made"* (John 1:1–3, NIV).

Some years later, I came to love the words of Isaiah 46:

> Bel bows down; Nebo stoops;
> Their idols are on beasts and livestock;
> These things you carry are borne
>   as burdens on weary beasts.
> They stoop; they bow down together;
>   they cannot save the burden,
>   but themselves go into captivity.
> (Isaiah 46:1–2, ESV)

Bel and Nebo were Babylonian gods. When Babylon was conquered by Persia, the people fled, carrying their idols on their already overburdened livestock. These idols couldn't save the people; they couldn't even save themselves, for the people had to carry and take them along into captivity. What a contrast this is to the God of Israel, who both saved and carried the Israelites through their trials and hardships. God still saves and carries us today.

Bel and Nebo are idols, while God is the living God. No idol, no friend, not even we can fully prepare ourselves for what is to come. But God is alive and well and working in our lives today. He can hear our cries and respond not only through the words of His book, the Bible, but also through the power of His living Spirit.

On Monday, June 18, 1990, I visited my doctor in the afternoon. I had six weeks left to go in my pregnancy and two weeks remaining in my school year. In a few days, I would have to write report cards for my students.

My doctor silently examined me, observing the continued swelling of my face and ankles due to my increased blood pressure. As she measured downwards across my abdomen, tracking the growth of the baby, we both noticed that the measurement had not increased from the week before. I could see the concern on her face as she rechecked the length of our baby.

The doctor informed me that I had toxemia and would need to stop work and go into the hospital for bed rest. I didn't object, but silently wondered at all of this.

That evening, after I packed my bag, my husband and I had supper and then headed across the city to the hospital. As we began our half-hour drive, I began to experience upper abdominal pains.

By the time we arrived at the hospital, I was in a great deal of pain. Attempts by the nurses to ask the usual questions upon admission failed miserably; all I could do was ask to sit down. Someone quickly provided a wheelchair, and shortly thereafter I was whisked upstairs. Any further admission questions must have been answered by my husband.

Things were a blur after that. The pain continued to worsen and the number of people involved in my care increased dramatically. My husband later said there had been as many as ten people in my room.

Before long, it became clear to the doctor in charge that I would need to give birth to our baby that night, otherwise one or both of us would not survive. My liver and kidneys were failing due to the toxemia which was now progressing quickly into preeclampsia. Both my life and the baby were at risk. They tried to induce me; however, this didn't produce strong enough contractions for a natural birth. So I was quickly prepped for a C-section.

As I was wheeled into the operating room, the attending nurse asked me what we planned to name our child. I wasn't so sure of our choice of a girl's name. The boy's name, on the other hand, I was quite positive about—we would call him Justin!

At 11:45 that night, Justin was born, six weeks premature and weighing only three pounds, seven ounces. The doctor discovered that my placenta was not properly attached. This flattened circular organ was there during pregnancy to supply our baby with oxygen and nutrients and, if unattached, would explain why he had stopped growing inside my uterus. Justin was whisked away to the Neonatal Intensive Care Unit.

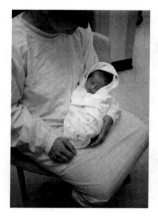

When I awoke from my anesthetic, I was taken down to see our son. He was a "doll"; the nurses said he was the cutest baby there. He had strawberry blond hair and big, big eyes that were a very dark blue, almost black. He had long, delicate fingers and my husband's mother, Nana, commented that he had a heart-shaped face. How fitting: "Monday's child is fair of face."

I was discharged after five days, but Justin needed to remain in the hospital for a total of six weeks, gaining weight slowly and requiring help to eat through gavaging (a method of feeding tiny preemies through a tube traveling down their throat and into their stomach). I worked hard to pump my breast milk for him to receive through the gavage, and later through a bottle. Once he was strong enough, I tried to breast-feed him. Finally, Justin reached a weight of five pounds and was allowed to go home, although he would continue to gain weight slowly and have trouble breast-feeding. As we left the hospital, I felt both relieved and nervous. Justin had been six weeks premature, and had spent that exact amount of time in hospital.

Years later, when Justin was about twelve years old, a friend from our church gave me a poem called "Heaven's Very Special Child." That same year, a second friend, also from our church, gave me the same poem with an article attached. Here is the poem and the attached newspaper article:

Dear Ann Landers: My husband is Dr. John A. Massimilla, pastor of the United Methodist Charge, Magnolia, Del. He is also chaplain for the Hospital for the Mentally Retarded in Stockley, Del. We have a severely retarded daughter.

A few years ago you printed a poem I wrote about such children. As a result, we received many letters from parents of retarded children, and have carried on a heartwarming correspondence with these parents—hopefully giving them comfort and reassurance.

The poem, "Heaven's Very Special Child," was written purely through inspiration from a greater power. We would like to share these words once again with your readers. It can mean so much if parents learn to see their retarded child as a blessing and a special person.

Sincerely, Mrs. Edna Massimilla

Hatboro, PA

HEAVEN'S VERY SPECIAL CHILD

A meeting was held quite far from Earth!
It's time again for another birth.
Said the Angels to the Lord above,
"This Special Child will need much love.
His progress may be very slow,
Accomplishment he may not show.
And he'll require extra care
From the folks he meets down there.
He may not run or laugh or play;
His thoughts may seem quite far away.
In many ways he won't adapt;
And he'll be known as handicapped.
So let's be careful where he's sent.
We want his life to be content.
Please, Lord, find the parents who
Will do a special job for You.
They will not realize right away
The leading role they're asked to play.
But with this child sent from above
Comes stronger faith and richer love.
And soon they'll know the privilege given
In caring for their gift from Heaven.
Their precious charge so meek and mild
Is Heaven's Very Special Child.

God had chosen me to be the mother of a very special child. *"Behold, children are a heritage from the Lord, the fruit of the womb is a reward"* (Psalm 127:3, NKJV). This was an honor for which I thank God. I thank Him, too, for how He prepared my heart to receive such a child.

What are your dreams? As a young wife, my dream was to be a mother; but what was typical in the eyes of our culture was not what God had in mind for me. His plan was for me to be the mother of a special child, who would require my constant care and attention.

Our first months at home with our new son were less than idyllic, as I was often questioned regarding whether our tiny baby was "getting enough" when he was breast-fed. I wanted so much for my child and I to benefit from the excellent nutrition and bonding that came with breast-feeding. However, because Justin had been labeled with "failure to thrive" while still in the hospital, many still worried about his slow weight gain. Unfortunately, this caused the breast-feeding to become somewhat stressful, which in turn hampered its success. Consequently, we sought the help of lactation consultants and a breast-feeding clinic. I did my best to continue with the breast-feeding for as long as possible.

As our son grew, albeit slowly, I found I was able to accept his unique needs and love him just the way he was. With all my heart, I wanted to give him the best care I could provide. We spent hours every day reading books, playing with toys, and listening to music. I also enrolled both of us in infant swim classes. As a result, books, music, and swimming became lifelong loves for our son.

Justin was always a happy, sociable guy, but as he grew in size strangers often stared at him, startled to see a big kid in a stroller, babbling away joyfully in his own private language. However, I saw that once people spent time with him, they were touched by his loving ways.

Sometimes we carry heavy burdens—like the loss of a relationship or a struggle with others. In my case, the health of my child could have been a very heavy burden. But rather than seeing Justin's condition as a burden, I was able to love and accept him just as he was. And because God had prepared me ahead of time, all this was a little easier.

Trying to make my son live up to the expectations of our culture wouldn't have worked. Instead, I needed to allow him to grow and develop at his own pace, and I needed to embrace what God had given me rather than what He hadn't given me. This meant letting go of the temptation to carry the ideal of a normal, healthy child in my heart. How quickly our ideals can become burdensome idols.

> Come to Me, all you who labor and are heavy laden, and I will give you rest. Take My yoke upon you and learn from Me, for I am gentle and lowly in heart, and you will find rest for your souls. For My yoke is easy and My burden is light. (Matthew 11:28–30, NKJV)

> Cast all your burden on the Lord,
> And He shall sustain you.
> (Psalm 55:22, NKJV)

A friend showed me an excellent way of looking at our circumstances. "Don't look at things with a preconceived idea of what they are supposed to look like," she said. "That way we set ourselves up for disappointments. But try to see and notice what is already there. Mountains do not obstruct the view; they *are* the view! If only we would change our perception and look at our life from a different perspective. Be content with what you see."

I am so grateful. Because God prepared me ahead of time, I was able to quickly accept my son's special needs and embrace the wonderful child God had provided, who loved us and taught us many lessons along the way. Justin was the vessel through which God was molding me. And God provided all that we would need, every step of the way!

CHAPTER TWO
God Is the Great Weaver

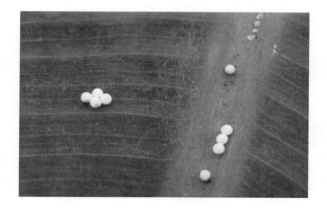

Listen to me, O house of Jacob,
all the remnant of the house of Israel,
who have been borne by me from before your birth,
carried from the womb.
                    —ISAIAH 46:3 (ESV)

You hem me in, behind and before, and lay your
        hand upon me.
Such knowledge is too wonderful for me; it is high;
        I cannot attain it.
                    —PSALM 139:5–6 (ESV)

2

Many threads are finely woven together to create a beautiful tapestry. Some are brightly colored, others are gold or silver, and finally, others are dark in hue. The Great Weaver forms our lives from all these threads. Some aspects of our lives are joyful, many are ordinary, and others are painful. But without each type of experience, our lives would not be deep and would not be truly His. Each thread adds to the beauty and richness of the tapestry of our lives.

After he was born, Justin remained in the hospital for six weeks due to his low birth weight and failure to thrive. During that time, I found myself swept into a new lifestyle, unfamiliar and absorbing. I drove back and forth to the hospital every day, held and fed my new baby, and looked around me at all the other needy babies in the hospital's Intensive Care Unit.

Because Justin was born premature and was gaining weight slowly, I found myself interacting with nurses and doctors in the hospital on a regular basis. Speaking on behalf of my son forced me to drop my shyness and become a more outspoken advocate for my child. I realized I was his voice, and the only one who could oversee all of his care. I found my life changed by that experience. God the Great Weaver was molding me into a stronger woman.

When Justin reached a weight of five pounds, his pediatrician discharged him from the hospital. We were finally allowed to take our little guy home. When he was about nine months old, I began attending a weekly program for new mothers at our local community health centre. Each week, a different speaker came to teach and assist us in our new role as mothers.

One week, the presenter was a child development specialist who oversaw the Early Childhood program at the Robin Hood Association for handicapped children. Her talk was for mothers with normally developing children and it included a thick handout on the stages of development for newborns and toddlers. I read through it carefully, wanting to know how my child was developing. Justin, who lay on the living room carpet beside me, was not yet rolling over.

After examining the pages of detailed information, I realized that something was wrong; Justin was clearly behind in his gross motor development, including such skills as rolling over and sitting up. I was concerned and gave her a call at her office. She offered to come out and do an assessment of my son's development. This assessment confirmed my thinking; Justin was significantly delayed and required special programming which the Robin Hood Association could provide. She enrolled Justin in their Early Intervention program.

We soon began to receive help from an Early Intervention worker who came into our home each week with helpful suggestions for how we could "boost" Justin's development. In addition, we received home visits from a highly trained occupational physiotherapist who gave us activities that would improve his gross motor development. For the next two and a half years, we received ongoing help from these professionals.

My favorite part of the Early Intervention program was the regular visits from this occupational physiotherapist. I loved working together as a team; I would show her the progress Justin had made over the past two weeks, and she would observe and set tasks for us to do on a daily basis for the next two weeks. These tasks always fit into Justin's daily routine. I paid attention to all the details of how he was positioned and to every little bit of progress he made. I poured my heart into those activities and celebrated every tiny sign of growth. I even began to chart the little bits of progress on a calendar.

God is the Great Weaver who weaves together the tapestry of our lives. He knew we needed help and He knew who could provide the very best help! The Robin Hood Association was right there in our home town, but I had never heard of them before that presentation at our community health centre. The Robin Hood Association became a part of our lives, woven into place by God's loving hands.

> Listen to me, O house of Jacob,
> all the remnant of the house of Israel,
> who have been borne by me from before
>   your birth,
> carried from the womb.
> (Isaiah 46:3, ESV)

> For you [God] formed my inward parts; you knit-
> ted me together in my mother's womb. I praise
> you, for I am fearfully and wonderfully made.
> Wonderful are your works; my soul knows it very
> well. (Psalm 139:13–14, ESV)

Another thread that God the Great Weaver wove into the fabric of our lives was a very unique genetic thread. When Justin was only seventeen months old, we were re-ferred to the Genetics Department at the University of Al-berta Hospital in Edmonton. Their hope was to determine the underlying cause of our son's delayed development. Little did we know that it would take more than five years of regu-lar visits before one of the geneticists, Dr. Stephen Bamforth, would discover a genetic cause for his condition. Justin was seven years old when a very small sample of his skin and blood was taken for testing. This led us to discover that there was something unusual about his X chromosome.

Dr. Bamforth contacted a man in Australia who was will-ing to test and examine these samples in his lab. By the time Dr. Bamforth received the results of this testing, we had moved from Edmonton to Calgary, Alberta. So he patiently explained the results to me over the phone.

Justin's blood and skin samples had been compared with blood samples taken from me. Both Justin and I had one X chromosome that was unusual. Males have one X chromo-some and one Y chromosome. Females, on the other hand, have two X chromosomes. One of my X chromosomes was normal, and the other was abnormal—whereas Justin only had one X chromosome, and it was abnormal. What made them unusual was an inversion (or flipped section) within the X chromosome. At one end of this inversion there was also some duplication of genes. It was very possible, Dr. Bamforth explained, that this "damage" could explain Justin's disability.

Further study revealed that all of the damaged X chromosomes in my blood sample were inactive or "shut off." It appeared this was a protection mechanism within my body. However, because Justin only had one X chromosome, it had to remain active and therefore fully affected him.

Dr. Bamforth further explained that if I were to conceive, I would have to use both my normal and my abnormal X chromosomes. By cell division, these would each contribute towards making a new X chromosome for my baby. This was how Justin received the abnormal X chromosome.

Later, when Justin was eleven years old, I remember sitting in a consultation room with him in the Alberta Children's Hospital in Calgary, ready to discuss his genetic history. Due to Dr. Bamforth's many phone calls and clear explanations, I was able to summarize my son's genetic uniqueness, and mine as well. The doctor was impressed.

But what really struck me in that consultation room was how clearly I saw God's hand on my life in all of this. God the Great Weaver had woven an unusual X chromosome into my body when I was conceived. Now, twenty-six years later, I had given birth to a little boy who also carried this chromosome, but who was far more affected by it than I was. Just as I know God heard my prayer and gave me a son with blue eyes, I know He chose me to be the mother of a very special boy.

God is a living God who already knows you because He formed you.

> Wonderful are your [God's] works;
> my soul knows it very well.
> My frame was not hidden from you,
> when I was being made in secret,
> intricately woven in the depths of the earth.
> Your eyes saw my unformed substance;
> in your book were written, every one of them,
> the days that were formed for me,
> when as yet there were none of them.
> (Psalm 139:14b–16, ESV)

> Know that the Lord, He is God;
> It is He who has made us, and not we ourselves;
> We are His people and the sheep of His pasture.
> (Psalm 100:3, NKJV)

> Listen to me, O house of Jacob,
> all the remnant of the house of Israel,
> who have been borne by me from before
>   your birth,
> carried from the womb.
> (Isaiah 46:3, ESV)

Are not two sparrows sold for a copper coin? And not one of them falls to the ground apart from your Father's will. But the very hairs of your head are all numbered. Do not fear therefore; you are of more value than many sparrows. (Matthew 10:29–31, NKJV)

I marvel at God's ability to weave together the tiny details of our lives and create the unique fabric of our existence here on earth. Thread upon thread, God wove together the unique tapestry of my life. Because of this one tiny chromosome, I would become a mother who would have trouble conceiving, who would have a miscarriage, and who would then have a special needs child. All of this would shape my life.

Justin's disability, in turn, shaped the lives of many people—his parents, those who taught him or cared for him, his classmates, friends, relatives, and teachers. All have been touched by his unique character. They have been touched, both physically by his little hands, and emotionally with his smile and simple unconditional love.

> And we know that in all things God works for the good of those who love him, who have been called according to his purpose. (Romans 8:28, NIV)

When Justin was only two years old, separation became a dark thread in my life when my husband chose to abandon our marriage for another woman. Little did I know that God would use that horrible struggle for good, as it caused me to reach out to Him.

After being a single mom for two years, my husband, who was an unbeliever, sought divorce. In God's eyes, mar-

riage is a lifelong commitment. Because I accept God's view
of marriage, it was very hard to live with the harsh reality of
my husband's unfaithfulness and the eventual divorce.

When Justin was five, I sought out a volunteer experience
where I could serve God and young people during the summer holidays. Because my son was developmentally delayed,
I wanted to volunteer at a summer camp where Justin would
receive good quality childcare. When I contacted Crowsnest
Lake Bible Camp in southwestern Alberta, I learned I could
work in the dining room for part of the day and still have lots
of time to spend with Justin. An elementary school teacher
was in charge of the childcare. This sounded like the camp for
us!

I worked hard and was blessed by my experience that first
summer at "Crow." But I must confess, I also had a hidden
agenda—I longed to meet someone special who loved God.

I didn't meet anyone that summer, but I did learn that I
needed to focus on serving and not dating prospects! So I surrendered the situation into God's hands and the next summer
I focused on serving Him. During my second summer at
"Crow," God brought someone special into the camp who
was a regular volunteer, and I was there helping in the dining
room when he arrived.

My supervisor, the camp cook, told me, "Dan is a good
man!" She explained that Dan had helped her with her car. (It
seemed she was also in the business of matchmaking.) Although I was shy about meeting someone new, especially
with so many others around watching, I found myself attracted to this tall, friendly man who was happy to have my
son sit on his lap while I worked in the dining room. Justin

was only three feet tall and thirty-four pounds at that time. He relied totally upon adults and caregivers to carry him or push him around in his big three-wheeled stroller, when he wasn't in his walker.

Dan and I went for a walk through the nearby woods one afternoon, picking wildflowers for the dining room tables. We talked on the beach in the evenings. God seemed to be saying that this could be the right man for me. When I saw my parents the next week, I excitedly told them I had met someone special.

Dan and I dated throughout the next year. I often wonder how we survived that year of dating, what with me being a single mom working two part-time teaching jobs, planning lessons, raising a special needs child, and keeping a home. Well, if Dan could withstand that amount of stress in our re-lationship, he could survive anything!

Dan and I married one year later. Right from the begin-ning, he understood that this special needs boy needed a full-time dad and embraced the fact that marriage would encom-pass all three of us. He truly was a good man! God the Great Weaver had now intertwined my life and Justin's with Dan's forever.

Fatherhood brought many new and difficult tasks into Dan's life, but he truly rose to the challenge. Justin, in turn, challenged Dan with his high needs, providing a crucible that lovingly shaped the life of his "Da."[1] Justin taught him to

---

[1] One of the questions that blended families have to deal with is, "What term do the children use to refer to their step-parent?" Shortly after Dan and I were married, as I tried to figure out what term Justin should use for Dan, it became apparent that Justin had come up with a

serve selflessly through helping with meals, changing diapers, and reading books at bedtime.

Dan remarked that such tasks required humility of Justin, as he had to accept the care of others in so many aspects of his life. We, in turn, learned to care for our son and love him under all circumstances—unconditionally. Justin taught us *how* to love others; Dan says this was his lesson and gift to all who cared for him.

God used Justin as a willing vessel. He was always one to love others easily; he accepted everyone with all their foibles and wrinkles and wasn't afraid to reach out to others and actually touch them in love. His love, like God's love for us, was unconditional, and because of this God could love others through Justin.

God molds us within the crucible of difficult circumstances. For some this is poverty, for many it is a trying relationship, and for others it is pain and suffering. But throughout all, God weaves the details of our lives into the lives of others and teaches us the lessons He wants us to learn along the way. The greatest lesson God has for us all is how to love.

In Jesus' day,

> a lawyer, asked Him a question, testing Him, and saying, "Teacher, which is the great command-

---

term of his own. Part of Justin's afterschool routine near the time that Dan would be arriving home from work was to look out our front room window onto the street. One day, Justin began to call out the word "Da" as Dan walked along the sidewalk and came in the front door. From that moment on, Justin's name for Dan was "Da." (This is a Scottish term for Dad, and being of Scottish heritage, it seemed a rather fitting term.)

ment in the law?"

Jesus said to him, "'You shall love the Lord your God with all your heart, with all your soul, and with all your mind.' This is the first and great commandment. And the second is like it: 'You shall love your neighbor as yourself.' On these two commandments hang all the Law and the Prophets." (Matthew 22:35–40, NKJV)

God wants us to learn to love Him and to love others just as we love ourselves. But we are self-centered people, and we naturally think of ourselves and our needs before others. But God's only Son, Jesus Christ, was a servant. In John 13, Jesus washed the feet of His disciples. God wants us to be just like that—willing to get down to serve and love others selflessly. But this is not an easy lesson to learn and we need lots of practice.

Justin provided just that—practice at learning to love, simply and unconditionally. He had many needs due to his disability. Whether he was eating a meal, going to the bathroom, getting into bed, or reading a book, he always required the help of a parent or caregiver. He was dependent upon others for just about every aspect of his day. And so, through these activities, we adults learned to serve selflessly and just *love*. Justin, in turn, reached out and loved back.

ᐱ   ᐱ   ᐱ

Another extraordinary example of God being the Great Weaver occurred when our son was fourteen years old. Dan,

Justin, and I were on our way to meet family at the Calgary Zoo. As we drove through our neighborhood, an unusual sound coming from the back seat caught our attention. We turned to see Justin struggling to breathe. Dan immediately pulled over to the curb and I jumped into the back seat.

We thought Justin was choking. I tried to help him but quickly realized that I was beginning to panic. So I told Dan we needed help and began to pray. Dan was already out on the curb, trying to flag someone down to assist us.

Unbeknownst to us, God the Great Weaver had placed us just where we needed to be at that moment. Each little thread was significant. Joe and his wife, people we had never met before, lived in a home about five blocks from our house. Their kitchen window overlooked the street where our van was pulled over to the curb.

That day, Joe and his wife and daughter were all at home having breakfast together, a fact that they later revealed was a bit unusual for their family. Their teenaged daughter was looking out the kitchen window as our van abruptly pulled to a stop at the curb and Dan jumped out, trying to call for help. Joe and his family quickly came out their back gate onto the boulevard to help us.

Now here is the amazing part! Joe is an epileptic, so he knows what a seizure is. He realized Justin was not choking but was having a grand mal seizure and asked us if our son had ever had seizures before. I said, "Not like this one! Justin has only had tiny petit mal seizures." Again, I said that I thought he was choking.

Joe was wise and didn't argue with me in my distraught state. He just asked if he could get Justin out of the car and

onto the grass beside the road. We quickly agreed. Joe went
to work with his wife at his side, who was encouraging him
with words such as, "Good job, Joe!"

I got down on my knees and prayed at Justin's side. Joe's
wife joined me. The two of us prayed out loud for him.

Finally, the seizure stopped and the ambulance arrived.
The seizure had only lasted for a few minutes, but it seemed
like an eternity. Justin was taken to the Children's Hospital
where we were told he had experienced a grand mal seizure,
the first one Dan and I had witnessed firsthand.

How thankful I was that God the Great Weaver had
placed us right outside that family's window and that their
daughter had been looking out at that very minute. Joe and
his family helped us through a situation that was totally for-
eign to us.

Only twenty-four hours later, Justin and I had to face a
second grand mal seizure, causing him to fall like dead
weight off the toilet onto the floor. Justin and I were alone
that day. But this time, thanks to Joe and his family, I knew
what to do. I remained calm and cradled Justin's head on a
towel, which kept him from injuring himself while the seizure ran its course.

How thankful I was for God's detailed care. Our God is a
God of little details. As it says in Ephesians 4:6, there is *"one
God and Father of all, who is over all and through all and in all"*
(ESV).

> The earth is the Lord's and the fullness thereof,
> the world and those who dwell therein. (Psalm
> 24:1, ESV)

God knew what He was doing! He was just weaving more and more intricate threads into the tapestry of our lives. Seizures would cause us to meet many other health professionals over the years as we sought help with this new situation. And Justin would touch and impact the lives of these people, too. They, in turn, would touch our lives, serve us, and become a part of the great and glorious tapestry God was creating through the life of our son.

THE WEAVER

My life is but a weaving between my Lord
and me,
I cannot choose the colors He worketh
steadily.
Oft times He weaveth sorrow, and I in foolish
pride
forget He sees the upper but I the under side.
Not till the loom is silent and the shuttles
cease to fly,
shall God unroll the canvas and explain the
reason why.
The dark threads are as needed in the
Weaver's skillful hand,
as threads of gold and silver in the pattern life
has planned.[2]

---

[2] Benjamin Malachi Franklin (1882–1965). U.S. Library Of Congress, Washington DC, Card #20060727210211. Information provided by grandson, Bob Corley

CHAPTER THREE
God Provides

Even to your old age I am he,
and to gray hairs I will carry you.
I have made, and I will bear;
I will carry and will save.

        —ISAIAH 46:4 (ESV)

For forty years you sustained them in the wilderness;
    they lacked nothing.

        —NEHEMIAH 9:21 (NLT)

3

Our God is an awesome God! He knows just what we need, even before we realize it. I saw this time and time again in our son's life.

At the time of my separation, when Justin was only two years old, God brought Linda into my life. We were introduced by a wonderful, caring neighbor. Linda invited me over for coffee and I discovered what a great listener she was. I told her that I had been asked to teach Sunday School in our church because of my training as a special education teacher. However, I didn't know the content of the Sunday School curriculum or the Bible. So how could I be a good Sunday School teacher?

Linda asked me, "How would you like to do a one-on-one Bible study?"

I agreed, and together we made plans to begin our study the next week.

A few days later, before I saw Linda again, I was at home feeling overwhelmed with sadness. While Justin slept in his crib, I cried because my husband was living elsewhere; I hated this separation and wanted my marriage back. But my husband wasn't interested in reconciliation; he was still involved with another woman.

My tears led me to cry out to God—something I had never done before. I simply asked Him to take me.

Whoosh! What felt like wind came from just a short distance away and rushed toward me, right into my chest! Later I realized that it had been the "wind" of the Holy Spirit. He had been right there in the room with me all along, and was now a part of me; I had become a new Christian. Immediately, I felt calm and my tears evaporated. I hadn't done anything to deserve God's saving grace and love; I had only chosen to cry out to Him with a sincere heart. In turn, He saved me out of the pit of my despair.

> Make Your face shine upon Your servant;
> Save me for Your mercies' sake.
> (Psalm 31:16, NKJV)

> Even to your old age I am he,
> and to gray hairs I will carry you.
> I have made, and I will bear;
> I will carry and will save.
> (Isaiah 46:4, ESV)

The very next day, when Linda walked into my living room for our first Bible study, she could immediately see something was different about me.

"Did something happen?" she asked.

I told her what had happened the night before. Linda was ecstatic! She understood God was working a change in me, healing and renewing me, and it was actually visible in the way I looked. Others noticed the change as well, including my husband. However, this did not cause him to reconsider the decisions he was making at that time.

God knew I was His child and He knew what I really needed—not only to learn the content of the Bible, but to reach out for God Himself. He knew, far more than I did, how much I needed *Him* in my life.

> And we know that in all things God works for the good of those who love him, who have been called according to his purpose. (Romans 8:28, NIV)

God provided not only support and friendship through Linda, but she also introduced me to a group of women who met weekly for a ladies' Bible study. These women cared about me and the turmoil and distress I was experiencing, caused by my separation. Their support and love was amazing!

Proverbs 3:5–6 was one of the verses we learned in that Bible study:

> Trust in the Lord with all your heart
> and lean not on your own understanding;
> in all your ways acknowledge him,
> and he will make your paths straight. (NIV)

These verses became "life verses" for me, and creating a simple tune I began to sing them each day. This was a great way to memorize these verses and make them a part of my daily walk. As I struggled in my role as a single mom, I sought God's help and called out to Him. In response, He gave me peace and direction.

I was able to stay home with our son that first year we separated. But the next year, with Justin entering his half-day class at Robin Hood's Early Childhood program, my ex-husband felt he should provide less financial support, as I would now be able to work part-time. I wasn't sure how I would do this, so I prayed specifically that God would provide a part-time job for me that would match my son's schedule.

Well, God provided just that! My sister-in-law did accounting work for The Heritage School, a private school for learning-disabled students. They were seeking a special education teacher who could work part-time hours. After interviewing with them, they chose to hire me. However, I was concerned about their request to start in April, three months before Justin was to embark on his first year in the Robin Hood program. I had hoped to begin teaching in September, but The Heritage School needed me right away.

I shared my concerns with the school's administrator and she immediately assured me that they would care for Justin in their Early Childhood program for the three months between April and June. Then, in September, he could begin the Robin Hood program, which was more suited to his level of development.

All this was so amazing! Not only did I have care for my son, but he would be just down the hall; we could even eat our lunches together! Although my job was full-time initially, when Justin entered his program in September it became part-time. God had provided just the hours I needed.

That fall, when I began teaching part-time, the pace of my life intensified even more, with staff meetings and responsibilities after school. But God provided the much-needed help of a young teen boy with a great deal of maturity who babysat for us.

In the meantime, God provided the next step in Justin's education through the Robin Hood Association. Their Early Childhood program was designed to help three- to five-year-olds who were delayed in their development. This half-day program took place in a special classroom within a regular elementary school. Physiotherapy and speech therapy were provided right there by two highly trained professionals who worked with the children and supported the classroom teachers and aides. We were blessed to have the very same physiotherapist who had visited our home for the past two years. It was a wonderful program!

Justin was one of six children who attended each morning. How odd it felt to put my small son onto a huge yellow bus each morning and watch him go off to school at the age of three! He was still very small for his age and could not walk unaided or speak more than a handful of words.

One of the aides in Justin's special classroom introduced me to her daughter, Alison, who became the first of many respite workers to care for our son over the years. We depended upon these people to help him with every aspect of his care—assisting him with eating, taking him for walks, and so much more. While these workers were with Justin, I got a much needed break from his ongoing care.

Through The Heritage School, I became friends with a speech-language pathologist on staff whose name was Susan.

One day, during a staff lunch at a local restaurant, Susan asked about the light she saw in my life. I was able to share with her my relationship with God and Jesus because of His light being reflected through me. As Ephesians 5:8 says, *"For you were once darkness, but now you are light in the Lord"* (NIV).

In time, Susan herself chose to have a relationship with Christ. God had provided such good mentoring and support when I was a young Christian that I knew she would also need this good foundation. So I gave her a Bible and we did a one-on-one Bible study together once a week for a year. Years later, she moved to a small town outside Calgary.

I met her again after I remarried and moved to Calgary. By then, Justin was seven. She invited me to be an assistant teacher for a Suzuki Early Childhood music program that she and her infant son were attending. I began attending this type of class with my son as well, and seeing the benefits for him chose to become a certified Suzuki Early Childhood music teacher. Suzuki music soon became a lifelong involvement for both Justin and me.

At the age of nine, Justin received a tremendous gift of communication. Throughout his entire life, he had struggled in this area and was only able to say about six different words. At this time, we were blessed to be receiving respite care from a young woman whose mother had a specialty in communication and had developed a system using pictures to represent words. For example, Justin could request a banana by putting a picture of a banana into our hand. We laminated and mounted these pictures on small squares of colored plastic. This made them strong and color-coded. Our son could use these cues, or pictures, to make requests and we, in turn, could use them to show him what he would be doing during the course of his day.

Justin became very adept at using these cues to tell us what he wanted to do. He became very expressive, too, with his body language. What a blessing it was that our son could finally, after nine years, express himself! God had provided an immense blessing through this woman and her daughter.

When Justin was twelve, I realized he needed something more in his day to challenge him and cause him to grow. I prayed for months that God would direct us. Through his school, we learned that Justin had a tremendous desire to play the piano which stood in the hallway near his classroom. So I began to pray that God would provide us with a piano. Well, He did just that! A used piano became available where I was teaching Suzuki music classes. My father agreed to help us with this purchase, and we had the piano delivered while Justin was at school. When he arrived home, we brought him into the living room where the piano stood. He was over-joyed! God had heard our prayers and, using many different people along the way, had provided our son with his own piano.

Piano quickly became a lifelong passion for Justin. He loved to play it almost every day, and always with pure joy! When he was away from home at his father's house, he loved to play his electronic keyboard. When he returned home, he would use his communication system to ask to play the piano right away!

It was difficult to find a Suzuki piano teacher who had experience teaching special needs students. Although I had Suzuki training to work with young preschoolers, I didn't have any training in teaching piano. After many unsuccessful phone calls, I bumped into the woman I had assisted in teaching my first Suzuki Early Childhood music class. It turned out she was also a piano teacher and had a student who was developmentally delayed. Although it was physically impossible to get Justin down the stairs into her basement for lessons, she invited me to observe her as she taught this other student.

So began my weekly commute across the city to attend these piano lessons. Afterward, I went home to apply what I had learned to my son's piano lesson time. We had to work patiently and repeat lessons many times, but it was well worth the effort! Justin was very committed and slowly began to imitate the notes and rhythms we practiced together.

One day, I decided to pursue the possibility of having our son take piano lessons with this teacher himself. I knew I couldn't get him into her basement, but God provided a solution. Three doors down from her house was a church that had an elevator and a piano! I introduced myself to the pastor there and explained our situation. We were able to arrange a time when Justin could come up the elevator into the church and use their piano for his lesson. My husband, Dan, made a wooden ramp to enable him to get onto the low stage where the piano stood. Each week, the pastor lifted this heavy wooden ramp into place and, for the first time, our son had his own lesson with his teacher.

Two years later, Dan and I had the sense that we needed to move across the city into an area closer to our church. God spoke to each of us separately, preparing us for this move. And yet, because of our own nervousness, it took three months before we realized He had prepared us with the same message.

The long, tedious search for a more accessible home for our son, who was now fourteen years old, was very stressful. But God encouraged us to be patient, and in the end He provided just the right home in an old neighborhood three blocks from the river, very close to our church and only five blocks from where Justin's piano teacher lived. From that time forward, we were blessed to have piano lessons in our own home. Again and again, God provided for all our needs.

Throughout our life, God has continued to provide for us—through supportive friends, wonderful jobs, very special schools, caring respite workers, and churches that have stood by us through it all. God has provided us with all the support and love we have needed.

So often, we think it is our job to provide for our own needs. Let's face it; our culture elevates those who are self-supporting and independent. But God wants to direct all the details of our life. Yes, He asks us to use our brain, and our own strengths and energy, too, but we need to lean on *His* wisdom and direction. Too often, we go ahead of God and miss His best for us. He has so many blessings in mind for us, if we will only pray and wait for His leading. In turn, God provides more than we could ever imagine.

> Oh, how great is Your goodness,
> Which You have laid up for those who
>   fear You,

Which You have prepared for those who
     trust in You
In the presence of the sons of men!
(Psalm 31:19, NKJV)

CHAPTER FOUR
God Blesses and Prepares

He makes me lie down in green pastures.
He leads me beside still waters.
He restores my soul.
He leads me in paths of righteousness for
    his name's sake.

—PSALM 23:2–3 (ESV)

Who is this King of glory?
The Lord, strong and mighty,
the Lord, mighty in battle!

—PSALM 24:8 (ESV)

4

God Blesses and Prepares through Wise Council

During the summer months of 2007, I took time to read a book that had been given to me by one of our respite caregivers. The book was called *Mitten Strings for God: Reflections for Mothers in a Hurry*, by Katrina Kenison. I read through this book during the quiet moments of my day. Her words spoke to me of my need to slow down and spend more quality time with my son.

Kenison writes:

> Like Thoreau, I love "a broad margin to my life"—the less packed into a day, the better. Sitting still, I am able to appreciate my life simply because I am taking the time to experience it. But even a few moments of tranquility can be hard won. It seems that idleness is suspect; we are supposed to be on the go. Perhaps that is why I am always so grateful for the small clearings that can suddenly appear even in the midst of a busy day. These accidental, hallowed scraps of time offer us a break from the outside world, at least for a few moments. Arriving ten minutes early for a piano

lesson, the boys flop down outside on a patch of fresh powder, waving arms and legs to etch a row of ragged angels into the snow. Informed that our pediatrician is running an hour behind schedule, we dash back out to the car, crawl into the back, and tell a story while rain pounds on the roof. Or someone suggests tea before bed, and we all gather round the table, light a candle, and drink in the night.

Having reaped the blessings of these accidental moments of grace, I am learning to leave some space around the edges of our days... In a society that endorses activity, I think we would all do well to put more trust in stillness.[3]

Kenison's book caused me to begin to examine my life and my tendency to always be doing something around the house. Whether it was preparing a meal, cleaning up, or making a phone call, I began to see that I was a mother who rarely sat still in her own home. Just as a page has a margin along its edge where there are no words, why couldn't my day have blank, unscheduled time so that I could "just be" with my son?

This was an ongoing lesson for me, not something I mastered quickly but rather something I needed to work on each and every day. I have learned from others that busyness is a common struggle. It can draw us away from spending quality time with our children, our spouse, our friends, and our God.

---

[3] Kenison, Katrina. *Mitten Strings for God: Reflections for Mothers in a Hurry* (New York, NY: Warner Books, 2000), pp. 23–24.

So when I caught myself rushing around the house, keeping busy, I learned to stop and make myself sit down with
Justin and "just be." I took a deep breath and looked around
at the blessings right there before my eyes! I found that
whenever I did this, Justin would bounce up and down in his
wheelchair with joy and wave his hands in the air with glee!
This was his way of saying, "Hooray, Mom!"

I have since thought that my son had wisdom beyond his
age, for here he was teaching me the value of just spending
time together, often just sitting quietly, doing nothing at all.
Some master this only after years of practice during inten-
tional meditation, or in retirement. But Justin learned this
skill at a young age, and thankfully he was patient in passing
it on to me. I still find it to be a daily struggle in a culture that
loves to keep busy, but by listening to God's promptings I am
learning the value of peace and stillness.

There are many who are always very hard at work with
one thing or another and think they are better for it or of
more value because of what they do. But I think there are
fewer who can say that they have learned to be at peace with
themselves without having to be doing something at the
same time. We have value because of who we are, not because of what we do. We are valuable in and of ourselves.

God's example of the perfect world was the Garden of
Eden. It wasn't until after "the Fall" that man had to work
and till the ground. The Garden of Eden was a perfect place
where man and woman could "just be" with God, at rest and
in relationship with Him.

Kenison also shares an interesting story about simplicity:

Two weeks before Easter, I visit a friend whose children are the same age as mine. When I arrive, she is just cleaning up after an afternoon of coloring eggs with her son and daughter. There are Ukrainian masterpieces, painstakingly created with special tools, dyes, and wax. In addition, they have made stenciled eggs, brilliant glitter eggs, and marbleized eggs, all from kits ordered from a catalog.

While the children head outside to play, my friend sweeps glitter off the floor, scrubs the table, and washes tiny paintbrushes. The results of their labors are breathtaking, and I ooh and ahh over every egg. They are beautiful. But, she confesses with a sigh, she has done most of them herself. The Ukrainian kit proved too complicated for the kids, and the stencils were difficult to do. The children each made a couple of glitter eggs, but they ended up with glue all over their hands and soon lost interest. "Next year," my friend says, laughing, "we're going back to the basic $2.99 kit from CVS!"

I think of those Easter eggs now as I set out to write about simplicity. So often, it seems, we are the ones who make our own lives more complicated than they need to be. We set the bar too high, take on too much, turn small doings into big ones. In part the culture is to blame—as each holiday rolls around, we confront an ever-expanding array of merchandise to go with it.

There is more to see, more to do, more to buy, than ever before. And how easy it is to fall into thinking that living well means partaking of all that's offered. With so many options and opportunities to choose from, it can be a challenge just figuring out where to draw the line.[4]

Kenison reminded me of the importance of simplicity when planning holidays, birthdays, or special activities. This has helped me not to miss valuable opportunities to achieve real meaning and to learn important lessons with my child. For example, focusing on singing "Happy Birthday to Jesus" with birthday cake and just a few gifts helped my son to learn the true meaning of Christmas. By keeping preparations and the event simple, both my child and I benefitted because I was less stressed and he was not overwhelmed. This meant we could both experience the joy of the moment and the real reason for our celebration.

Sadly, our culture often sees costly and elaborate events as better than simple, well-chosen details that will teach our children sensitivity and respect. A friend of mine has taught her daughters to open each birthday gift they receive as soon as a friend or relative arrives at their home. This has helped her girls to focus on each person and their gift, to thank them individually, and to not get greedy or overwhelmed by one gift after another.

And now a short story about Kenison's son, Jack:

---

[4] Ibid., pp. 34–35.

Now Jack is coming home from kindergarten, his pockets full of rocks to be turned into gold, and sandwich crusts to leave on the hearth for the hungry brownie who creeps out each night for a secret snack. Jack offers daily progress reports on his own loose tooth, eager to make the passage into his older brother's society of gap-toothed grins and quarters under the pillow. But I am in no hurry to see him go. For now I'm content to let him renew my own sense of magic and wonder. Emptying his pockets over the washing machine at night, I am reminded of the endless possibilities he sees before him as he makes his way in the world each day, of the magic he still knows to be the truth.[5]

My reading of this book caused me to contemplate my own life. Do I take time to *really* listen to my child when he wants to tell me about his day? Do I allow myself to become absorbed in the things which absorb him? And finally, do I let my child truly be himself?

God blessed me through Kenison's book immensely, and because I took her words to heart, I can look back on all the special times I had with my son with great thankfulness. Sometimes God uses the wisdom of an author, speaker, or teacher to guide us. In my case, the timing was especially poignant in light of the huge change that was about to happen in my life.

---

[5] Ibid., p. 145.

God Blesses and Prepares through Scripture

In the fall of 2007, God directed me to read to Justin from Isaiah 46 during our morning devotional time. This was a precious quiet time of prayer and reading that we enjoyed each day while waiting for his school bus.

Each morning, I would let him choose which activity we would do first: read the Bible or pray. Sometimes he would get visibly excited when I read to him from the Bible, bouncing up and down in his wheelchair seat. When it was time to pray, Justin would choose from a tray of photos of people he knew, and we would take turns praying for that person.

I was thankful for God's leading in what we should read each day. But what continued to surprise me was the fact that day after day, over the next three months, God directed me to read aloud to Justin from Isaiah 46. Sometimes I would question this, thinking surely we should move onto another passage of Scripture, but God quietly assured me that this was fine and not to worry. God uses my strong visual sense to enable me to visualize the words He wants to communicate to me. This may sound strange, but I literally saw the words as if they were on a blackboard.

So Justin and I continued to read from Isaiah 46 each morning. Some days, we would meditate on one verse. At other times, we would focus on two or three verses. Some of the verses were powerful and moving. Other verses seemed strange at first, causing me to stop and think about how they applied to us. Often I felt like I was an officer in the army reading a moving speech to his troops. I found the words caused my heart to stir and my back to straighten. I read the verses in a strong and commanding voice to my son.

I didn't realize until months later that God was using Isaiah 46 to bless and prepare me for what was to come.

Here are the words of Isaiah 46:

> Bel bows down; Nebo stoops; their idols are
> on beasts and livestock;
> these things you carry are borne as burdens
> on weary beasts.
> They stoop; they bow down together; they
> cannot save the burden,
> but themselves go into captivity.

> "Listen to me, O house of Jacob, all the rem-
> nant of the house of Israel,
> who have been borne by me from before
> your birth, carried from the womb;
> even to your old age I am he, and to gray
> hairs I will carry you.
> I have made, and I will bear; I will carry and
> will save.

> To whom will you liken me and make
> me equal,
> and compare me, that we may be alike?
> Those who lavish gold from the purse, and
> weigh out silver in the scales,
> hire a goldsmith, and he makes it into a god;
> then they fall down and worship!

They lift it to their shoulders, they carry it,
they set it in its place, and it stands there; it
     cannot move from its place.
If one cries to it, it does not answer or save
     him from his trouble.

Remember this and stand firm,
recall it to mind, you transgressors,
remember the former things of old;
for I am God, and there is no other;
I am God, and there is none like me,
declaring the end from the beginning
and from ancient times things not
     yet done,
saying, 'My counsel shall stand,
and I will accomplish all my purpose,'
calling a bird of prey from the east,
the man of my counsel from a far country.
I have spoken, and I will bring it to pass;
I have purposed, and I will do it.

Listen to me, you stubborn of heart,
you who are far from righteousness:
I bring near my righteousness; it is not
     far off,
and my salvation will not delay;

I will put salvation in Zion, for Israel
     my glory."
(Isaiah 46:1–13, ESV)

Now read it one more time, but this time I suggest you read it aloud with a mighty, powerful voice!

My thoughts/paraphrase:

> The small "g" gods are weak and useless!
> They cannot speak silently into your heart.
> They cannot save or rescue you!
> They must be carried and lifted onto your
>   back.
> Just another burden to bear.
>
> But the God of Israel is strong and mighty!
> Far from being immobile like a statue, or idol,
> He is ready to carry, ready to bear.
> He is the King of glory!
>
> This God is the Lord of salvation.
> Who can you possibly compare Him to?
> He has been there, wooing you from before
>   your birth.
> He will direct your path all your life, even
>   unto death.
>
> Have you forgotten what He has done for
>   you?
> How He saved you?
> Where are your eyes today?
> What fills your mind and takes you away
>   from God?

Fill your heart with the goodness and truth of
    the Lord.
Fill your eyes and mind and heart with Him.
He has a plan and purpose for your life.
He is bringing all these things to pass.
He is the mighty King of glory!

I read Isaiah 46 aloud to Justin again and again, and the
words moved me and began to take root in my heart. These
were God's words, spoken to His people, and now spoken
directly to me, His child.

God is very much alive and well today, for He is the living God. The Bible is His living Word, which speaks to each
of us directly, convicting, encouraging, and teaching.

God Blesses and Prepares through the Holy Spirit

God also chose to bless and prepare me through a wonderful
change that happened in Justin that same fall. Justin had always been one to hold my hand in a loving way, and I had
always loved to give him hugs and kisses, which he was very
good at receiving. But that fall, for the first time, he began to
give me both hugs and kisses on his own initiative. These
were big and very loving. If he wanted to give me a hug, he
would grab the shoulder of my shirt and pull me into his
chest.

At first, considering Justin's delayed development, I was
concerned that if he started to do this at school it might become inappropriate and cause problems. In the way I had
learned to trust, God told me not to worry. Rather He en-

couraged me to teach my son to be gentle, and to lean into those hugs and receive the immense love.

Day after day, Justin would come home from school and, before he took off his jacket, he would give me a big kiss on the cheek. After taking off his jacket and getting settled, he would invariably reach out for my right shoulder and pull me into his chest for a big hug.

I learned that these were gifts I needed to receive from my son. And in time, I realized that while leaning on Justin's chest I could feel God's love envelop me, and often tears would come to my eyes.

I look back on those hugs and kisses now and realize God was giving me an immense blessing that would come to mean so much more in only a few months' time. An elderly friend later caused me to consider that God might have also been preparing Justin ahead of time. Maybe that was why, all of a sudden, he began to give his mother daily hugs and kisses!

God Blesses and Prepares through Words of Knowledge

In December 2007, Dan and I celebrated Christmas together, setting aside Justin's gifts for when he returned from spending Christmas with his father. However, when we brought him home on December 31, it was apparent that he was sick with a cold.

Justin wasn't one to fight a cold easily. He loved to stay in bed and sleep it off, which was often the best thing. So this was what he did. I had hoped to celebrate Christmas with him right away, but those plans could surely wait another day.

Our tradition was to use the symbol for "birthday" and open presents to celebrate Jesus' birth, followed by chocolate birthday cake and all of us singing "Happy Birthday to Jesus." The top of the cake was decorated with a tiny figurine of Baby Jesus. I would also reinforce this with a variety of Christmas stories, including ones about the birth of Christ, in the weeks approaching Christmas.

The following day, I asked Justin if he was ready to celebrate with us, holding out the bright yellow symbol for birthday. I was surprised by his answer; Justin put the cue for birthday into his communication box, indicating that he didn't want to do it right now. He cuddled back down under his covers, showing me his desire to stay in bed.

Well, now I really knew he was sick. It wasn't like Justin to refuse a birthday celebration, complete with chocolate cake. And so he spent that day in bed, waking only to drink or eat his meals.

This continued for an entire week. Each morning, I would hope for the chance to open presents with Justin and sing "Happy Birthday to Jesus." But each day he was too sick to get out of bed. So we continued to bring him his meals and care for him there, as my hopes of celebrating Christmas with Justin that year waned.

On Saturday, January 12, 2008, only a week later, I sent out the following email to our family and friends:

Hello to all of you,

I type this at a strange hour of the morning—3:30 a.m.—as I woke in the middle of the night and thought I should do something beneficial with my wakefulness. So I am writing to all of you. It was good to get some sleep tonight in my own bed, as Justin's father and step-mother are now at the hospital with him. And yes, I will go back to bed again after typing this letter.

Justin is very unwell. He became sick on December 31 with a cold or flu. Initially it seemed he was just a very tired guy who couldn't get out of bed. But about four days later, he also developed a runny nose. By Monday, January 7, this was a green, runny nose that needed antibiotics. He could no longer take in fluids very well and he had a fever, so we knew we needed to take him into the Emergency Department at the Children's Hospital, where he was diagnosed with a sinus infection. They gave Justin one strong dose of IV antibiotics late Monday night in "Emerg" and sent us home with a prescription for an oral antibiotic.

But the fever wouldn't go away and the sinusitis didn't improve. Having spent the next two days at home, on Thursday morning his fever was so bad and he was so sick that he couldn't drink anymore. So I knew we had to take Justin back into the hospital. He spent all day Thursday in "Emerg" with doctors and nurses bustling about him, as he was a very sick young man. He was diagnosed with pneumonia on top of his sinusitis.

At supper time on Thursday, he was admitted and given a bed on a ward upstairs, and received excellent care from the nurses and doctors there. (This was the same ward he was on only a month ago, when he had blood in his urine and was diagnosed with a urinary tract infection.)

Yesterday morning (Friday), Justin took a turn for the worse and began to have trouble breathing. His heart rate and blood pressure were up, too. He began to go septic (acidic), which meant that the infection had moved from his lungs into his blood. So they moved him very quickly and with much accompanying medical staff—nurses, a doctor beside his rolling bed, and a respiratory tech holding his oxygen mask, who rode on the bed beside him. You start to get the picture—we were getting excellent care and they were very concerned about Mr. Justin.

All of us, as one team, moved Justin down to the ICU (intensive care unit). There were so many wonderful people literally staying right by his side that when I saw how crowded the elevator was, I almost took the next one with Justin's empty wheelchair and luggage. But the doctor wouldn't hear of it, so we left the wheelchair in the hallway instead. It was a funny but special moment to know how much we were loved and cared for, revealing that Justin and I were the priority, not our belongings.

Justin is still in intensive care, where he has his own nurse and the almost constant care of a specialized ICU doctor. He is a tiny bit more stable. But he is not termed "stable" by any means. What I mean is that he is now sleeping a lot and his heart rate is steady. His oxygen levels are stable most of the time, as he is now on a CPAP (Constant Positive Air Pressure) breathing mask that gives him oxygen, since he is not able to get enough on his own. He continues to be on more than one IV antibiotic for his sinusitis and pneumonia. But the doctors are very concerned about Justin. Today, Saturday, they will tell us more, as we hope to see him improve and stabilize further, slowly, step-by-step.

Justin's father just updated me further saying that the doctors are now calling this an acute lung injury. Pneumonia is the main underlying cause. (You might also get an acute lung injury from inhaling chemicals. However, this is not Justin's situation.) In his case, the inflammation in his lungs has led to infection, which leads to more inflammation, which has become a vicious cycle. Justin had an x-ray last night. They brought a portable machine to his ICU bed so that they didn't have to move him. This revealed that his pneumonia had worsened.

The good news is that Justin's vital signs—blood pressure, heart rate, oxygen saturation—have improved.

One Special Story:

I know all of this is special, but I have to tell you the little story of our first visitor to Justin's bedside yesterday (Friday) in the ICU. Justin's school principal came to visit with a homemade card in her hand from Justin's classmates, teacher, and aides. She is a tall, striking woman with beautiful white hair. She has known Justin for many years. Before becoming the principal of Justin's current school, she was also the principal of his previous school.

She is a wonderful lady and she had a very meaningful and special visit with Justin, who for the first time in hours tried to use his voice—very softly—when she squatted down and talked to him. It really sounded as if he was quietly singing, and Justin's principal said this as well. He also reached out his hand, taking it out from under his hot little body where he had cuddled his hands, and reached out to her. They held hands for a moment, and then Justin cuddled his hand back under his chest. It was beautiful!

I thought of some of you over the past 24 hours:

Tessa [one of my nieces], I thought of you in your role as a nurse as I looked across Justin's tired body yesterday at a very young, focused nurse who works on the ICU with children of varying ages, sizes, and illnesses. Her name was Ashley, and she is in her twenties. She was great!

Stephanie [another of my nieces], I thought of you yesterday because the nurse in charge of Justin's care in the "regular" ward where we stayed for about twelve hours before going to the ICU was also named Stephanie. She is a young, cheerful nurse who also cared for him at the end of November. She quickly identified an error regarding Justin's care on Thursday evening and was very dedicated, giving up all her other patients when he got significantly worse the following morning.

Emily [another of my nieces], it was you who saw Justin the most recently, and who spoke so beautifully to him as you always do. He was very sick when you came to our home, only one day before he went into "Emerg" the first time, this past Monday. Much has happened since then.

Many of you have been on my mind lately. And we love you all. And thank you, each one of you, for your support and love. And if Justin could say hi, he would!

Love, Diane.

After writing that email, I did go back to bed and got some more sleep.

That afternoon, God chose to prepare both Dan and I at the very same moment while we were on either side of

Justin's hospital bed. Amongst the sounds and sights of many machines and tubes and more medical care than I had ever witnessed firsthand before, God chose to tell both of us separately the very same message: "Justin might not make it."

When Dan received this message, not knowing that I had received the same words, but knowing how serious it was, he immediately thought, *God, there is no way I am going to tell Diane this!* After spending a few hours with Justin in ICU, we went home, leaving him to visit his father and step-mother. On our way home, we talked about our son and his condition. Suddenly, I said to Dan, "You realize how serious this is, don't you?" At that point, we discovered that God had given each of us the same message that "Justin might not make it."

I wasn't surprised that God had chosen to prepare us with the same phrase at the same time. He had done this once before when He was preparing us to sell our home and move across the city. This is how God has worked in our lives. He wants to prepare us and He prepares us well. He knew that this was an important message. He was not asking Dan to take on the burden of telling me this terrible news; God took care of all these details Himself.

Later that same evening, Dan contacted the Associate Minister from our church, who came to our home right away. While the three of us prayed together about Justin, God chose to prepare me even further by giving me the word "Heaven." At that point, I was at peace and believed fully that this was where God was taking our son.

For this is God, our God forever and ever;
He will be our guide even to death.
(Psalm 48:14, NKJV)

God also gave me the words "will" and "willing" and the sense that we needed to be at peace with His will and be a willing part of what He was doing. When I look back on this time, I see just how stunning this was; it was as if I was a soldier receiving orders from my captain. I felt strong and ready to go forward into battle. I can only give God the credit for this, for I loved Justin deeply and can't see any other reason for my calm strength.

That evening, I felt I should phone my longtime mentor and prayer partner. She had been receiving our emails and was already praying for us. When I told her the messages we had received from God, she said that she, too, had the sense from God that Justin was being taken heavenward. This was so confirming and gave me an even greater peace.

Once God told Dan and me that "Justin might not make it" and had given me the word "Heaven," I felt our job was to trust that God was in control and would bring about His very best for all of us. We didn't know exactly what that would look like or how long it would take; we only knew we needed to rest in God's will. So we asked friends and family to pray for God's will and for us to rest in that will.

Why was it so important to us that our friends and family pray in that manner? Sometimes we pray and pray for what we want, ignoring the fact that this may not be what God wants for us. Sometimes God relents. But in the end, we don't receive God's best blessing. Rather, we receive what we wanted.

An example of this is when the Israelites prayed and asked God to give them a king (1 Samuel 8:1–22). Other surrounding nations had kings, but Israel at that time did not. God gave the people what they wanted, knowing the people were rejecting Him as their true king. God warned the Israelites through His prophet Samuel that this king who would reign over them would take their sons and appoint some to his armies and some to plow his fields. Their king would take their daughters to be his servants. He would also take a tenth of their sheep. But the people would not heed God's warning; they were determined to have their way, which they thought was best.

In Justin's case, I was concerned that if we didn't pray for God's will, which we knew to be His best for all, we would have to settle for something much worse which we might eventually regret terribly. We felt it was time to put shoe leather to our faith and walk it out, not just talk about it. The bottom line was, did we trust that God knows best?

Scripture tells us of a good king, King Hezekiah of Judah, who

> was sick and near death. And Isaiah the prophet, the son of Amoz, went to him and said to him, "Thus says the Lord: 'Set your house in order, for you shall die, and not live.'" Then [Hezekiah] turned his face toward the wall, and prayed to the Lord... [and] wept bitterly. (2 Kings 20:1–3, NKJV)

God heard Hezekiah's prayers and relented, letting him live for fifteen more years. But Hezekiah later had a son, named Manasseh, who reigned after he died and was a very evil king. He, in turn, raised a son, named Amon, who was also an evil king.

What if Hezekiah had let God take him at his appointed time? God let Hezekiah live because of his pleading, but the end result had far-reaching consequences that affected many.

Dan and I needed to *"trust in the Lord with all your heart and lean not on your own understanding; in all your ways acknowledge him, and he will make your paths straight"* (Proverbs 3:5–6, NIV).

Within the first couple of days of Justin being in the ICU, God brought Isaiah 46 to our minds again through the caring words of two special people. One was Dan's brother, Ian, who quoted from Isaiah 46:11—*"I have spoken, and I will bring it to pass; I have purposed, and I will do it"* (ESV).

The other was through a friend who came to the hospital, bringing with her a card, in which she quoted Isaiah 46:4.

> Even to your old age I am he, and to gray hairs I will carry you. I have made, and I will bear; I will carry and will save. (ESV)

Again, God was using Scripture to prepare us.

When I look back on this time, I am always amazed by the peace I felt. This peace was noticeable to many of our friends and family, but they didn't always recognize the source and it was often hard for me to explain that my peace and strength was not of this world; it was due to God and His hand upon me.

Some also wondered at my apparent lack of tears. I did have tears, but they usually came when God prompted me to lie down. Then the tears would come, gently at first, then heavier, like waves crashing on a beach.

> Hear my cry, O God; attend to my prayer.
> From the end of the earth I will cry to You,
> When my heart is overwhelmed;
> Lead me to the rock that is higher than I.

> For You have been a shelter for me,
> A strong tower from the enemy,
> I will abide in Your tabernacle forever;
> I will trust in the shelter of Your wings. Selah

> For You, O God, have heard my vows;
> You have given me the heritage of those who
>   fear Your name.
> (Psalm 61:1–5, NKJV)

I thank God that the tears never overcame me or filled me with total despair. I would grieve heavily for a time, but then the tears would subside. God would then enable me to go through the next hour of talking to doctors, friends and family, or other parents who were dealing with a health crisis in their child's life, too, there at the Children's Hospital. Rather than being filled with fear, panic, or worry, God filled me with His incredible peace and strength to stand firm—in the moment—in Him and with Him.

> May the God of hope fill you with all joy and peace as you trust in him, so that you may over-

flow with hope by the power of the Holy Spirit.
(Romans 15:13, NIV)

The preparation God had given us ahead of time meant everything to me, because I knew what God was doing and where He was taking our son. I could begin to grieve and say the words I needed to say to Justin. How thankful I was to have ten days in the hospital to be quiet, to pray, to journal, and to cry. This was only possible because we had been prepared beforehand.

The stronger, harder waves of grief would come later. But for now, God had given me what I needed for that time and place.

Our God is an amazing God! He speaks to us in many ways in order to prepare us for His will and plan. Firstly, God speaks to us through the wisdom of His Scriptures. Secondly, He sometimes chooses to speak through the counsel of a wise person, whether directly or through a book or article. God can also prepare us through the loving touch of another person. Finally, God may choose to give us messages involving pictures, words, or phrases.

Without these different acts of preparation God graciously gave us, I can't imagine how we could have fully accepted what was happening to our beloved son. We consider all this a gift from God, who blessed and prepared us ahead of time. God is able to bless and prepare us for any difficult struggle or situation.

CHAPTER FIVE
God Draws Us Forward

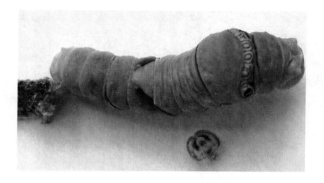

To whom will you liken me and make me equal,
and compare me, that we may be alike?
　　　　　—ISAIAH 46:5 (ESV)

To everything there is a season,
A time for every purpose under heaven.
　　　　　—ECCLESIASTES 3:1 (NKJV)

5

God was gently moving us forward as He unfolded His plan for our lives. It was Sunday, January 13, and Dan and I were able to attend church in the morning before joining the others who were visiting Justin in the ICU. He had now been in hospital for four days, and God continued to give us peace that He was taking our son to heaven in His time.

However, I was not prepared for the words that were spoken by our Anglican priest that morning. I gasped in surprise when he told us God had given one of the members of our congregation a vision of a dove hovering over the front, left-hand side of the sanctuary that then settled on the altar at the front. The front, left-hand side of the church was where we always sat with Justin on Sundays, as there was room there for people in wheelchairs.

Our Anglican church was quite evangelical and had a custom of recording any images or words that were received by the prayer team before each service. These images or words were then shared with the congregation just before communion. This Sunday, however, was a bit unusual in that this image of the dove was shared early in the service. It seemed almost as if a news bulletin had been read aloud to everyone there that morning.

Later, at the usual time, a message was read to the congregation that had been received from God that morning by the prayer team. It was an image of an hourglass lying on its side and the words, "There must be change; you can't stay as you are."

These words may have spoken to several people in our congregation that morning. But for me, I felt these words were speaking to my heart and encouraging me to be ready for change. Huge change! God had told me He was taking my only remaining son to heaven. This would have a huge impact on my life, for most of my waking moments had been taken up with loving and caring for my son.

Dan and I went over to the prayer vestibule to receive prayer. We were joined there by our priest, who knew the seriousness of Justin's condition, as well as Betty and Ted, a couple who had prayed for Justin and me in the past.

When Betty began to pray for me, she immediately saw a dove hovering over and between Dan and me. Her husband shared with us his sense that Justin knew he was loved by all his parents, and by God. He asked me if I had verbalized my release of my son into God's hands. He also asked whether or not I knew that God's hands are perfect.

At that point, our priest, who was standing close beside us, received the word "tenderly" from God, which he shared out loud with us. I had a sense of Justin being held tenderly in God's hands. I was encouraged by Betty to hand him over physically with my outstretched hands (and in my mind) into Jesus' hands and to release the mother-child bond. She then saw a bright light around Justin's bed. After we prayed and I had said my prayer, releasing my son into God's hands, she saw Justin free from his hospital bed and free from his wheel-chair. His upper body was surrounded by light and his face was looking up into the light with a real sense of physical freedom. She also sensed he was not afraid and that he felt God's peace.

Following the service, we returned to the hospital to be with Justin. But the words we had heard from God—"There must be change; you can't stay as you are"—seemed to linger and foreshadow what was soon to come.

Only four days later, I felt the Holy Spirit reinforcing this by putting into my mind the words, "Go forward. Leave." I felt God was telling me again that I could not stay in the past, nor could I hang onto Justin.

God is our commander-in-chief and I felt as if these words—"Leave" and "Go Forward"—were my marching or-ders. I knew implicitly that God loved me and was working all things out for good. These words came to me on a re-peated basis throughout the remainder of Justin's hospital stay; they became an ongoing message of encouragement and direction from God minute-by-minute, day-by-day.

This is not to say that I wanted to see Justin go, for he and I were very, very close and I loved him dearly. Nor is it to say that we did anything to stand in the way of the meticu-lous and caring work of the ICU medical staff, as they worked so hard to bring him back to us. Rather, we just stood there in the midst of what God was doing and tried to be a willing part of His plan.

The following day, while Justin continued to labor, God gave Dan the phrase "at play in the fields of the Lord." That same day, He gave me a picture in my mind of a field of thick green grass. What a joyful message to receive, pointing our hearts toward Justin's ultimate destination!

Due to the seriousness of our son's condition and the preparation we had received from God, Dan and I felt that we had to let family members, respite workers, and school staff know the truth of Justin's situation. We did not want to stand in the way of anyone who might want to visit him, especially knowing these visits might be their last.

On Saturday, January 19, I sent out another email to friends and family, hoping to communicate openly about our son's condition:

> Yesterday was a day in which Justin seemed more peaceful and less agitated. This was reflected in the fact that his blood pressure was up from the day before and was more like what it should be. However, his heart rate continues to be very high. In addition to this, Justin's breathing was poor and, as a result, they had to increase the oxygen concentration he was receiving from 45% to 100%. Justin had an EEG yesterday, indicating to the doctors that he was not having any seizures.
>
> What does all this really tell us? Well, I think all of this is a reflection of the fact that Justin is getting a lot of medical care and support. In some ways, we see improvement. But in other ways, we know this is an up and downhill journey. I am not wanting to sound discouraging, or even encouraging, but rather I want to be sensitive to all

of you who are reading this and are looking for bright glimmers of hope in what I write. And yes, there are little improvements, but there are also little setbacks, too. The reality is that Justin continues to be in very serious condition. So rather than paint a picture one way or the other, I think we have to be prepared to be at peace not only with what he is going through, but also we need to be patient with the fact that God is in control. And right now this is going slowly, and we need your prayers and encouragement for all, especially Justin and his parents.

Just think, our dear son has to lie in bed, unable to move, and when he worries or fights what God is doing his blood pressure dips low, which is unhealthy for him. So he has to rest, trust, and not fight against the machines, tubes, and care he is being given around the clock. He needs to trust and know that God is in control and, knowing that God loves him, Justin needs to just rest in that. Let's face it, Dan and I are not in control, and neither is Justin!

And so we continue forward, not knowing what the next day will hold, but that we are loved by all of you, and by our great God. The truth is that maybe we need to look at the good that is being brought out of this, for good can often come out of difficult times. Maybe this good is the love that I see being poured out as a result of Justin's illness. We are receiving many well-wishes from all of you. We know there are many prayers being offered up for us. Some of you have been able to visit and are sharing your love that way. Others are sending a card or an email of support and love. But all of you are caring, supporting, and showing your love for us. And on behalf of the three of us, I want to say thank you for all your loving thoughts and prayers.

With love in return,

Diane, Dan, and Justin

Later, the words of a friend were sent to us in an email:

We continue to wrestle with this ourselves, praying a Gethsemane kind of prayer for you in your agony. Not any of our wills, but His be done. Seems simplistic from folks outside of the situation. But the only way we know how to pray.

That evening, a dear friend of ours who had done respite care and housekeeping for us, came to visit our son. Having just experienced a difficult day, she was so blessed by Justin as she received a profound sense of peace from him during their visit. She also had the sense that God was doing something new in me.

As I left the hospital, heading home with the hope of getting some sleep, I noticed a light green color shining from the round lamps along the circular driveway at the front doors of the hospital. I paid for my parking and then headed for my car. As I left the hospital, the street light shone green, urging me forward. And then another green light, and another. I felt God urging me to phone a dear friend and prayer partner on my cell phone. I reached her at home and we talked and prayed, and I shared my observation of the color green on my way home. She looked up the words "grass green" and discovered the following definition: "life, abundant in nature, growth, renewal, health, self-respect, well-being. Green is the most restful color." I pondered this, thinking of how I felt God was urging me forward into a totally new life.

On Sunday, January 20, while we were in church and our son was still in the hospital, a woman in the congregation received a word picture from the Lord, a picture of angels and Justin, and a sense that he was crying out in his desire to be with the angels right now!

Although this word picture was given to us seven days later, these words came to mean a great deal to me in the months ahead. For January 20 was the day on which the doctors realized there was nothing more they could do; Justin had been given intense treatment for nine days and he had not responded.

We realized that God's plan was not to be thwarted. We remembered the words He had given us: "Justin might not make it," "Heaven," and "Leave and go forward."

Dan and I told the doctor in charge at the ICU that we had been expecting this moment ever since God had spoken to us and prepared us ahead of time. As we explained this to her, she nodded her head, saying that she was a Christian, too. She said she needed to hear such things and be reminded of God's control in all of this. We then had a meeting with her and Justin's father and step-mother to discuss how we wanted to handle his terminal condition.

I felt overwhelmed and rushed by the finality of the decisions made in that meeting. Inwardly, I had been hoping that God would determine the exact moment when Justin would go to heaven. When the meeting was over, I told everyone there that I needed to go down to Justin's room and asked that only my husband be in that consultation room when I returned.

As I walked down the hall to Justin's hospital room, I knew I needed time alone, but in a way I also needed to be with my son. But when I got to his room, it seemed empty. Justin's body was there in the hospital bed, but there were no words from him or the Holy Spirit. All seemed quiet. I had been convinced it was very important for me to be there in his room, but now I wasn't so sure. It seemed there was nothing left to do, no words to say, only a sense that I needed to listen to God.

"Leave and go forward," God said. "Leave and go forward." And so I put one foot forward, and then the other, and left the room and went back down the hall to where Dan was waiting. I had a sense that it was time to follow my husband, who had said only moments earlier that it was time for us to leave the hospital.

And so we did. Dan and I left the hospital at midnight and went for a moonlit drive in the countryside west of the city. I love the moon, and that night there was a full moon and clear sky. The moon reflected off the snow, creating a wonderful white scene before us as we drove through the foothills west of Calgary.

"Washed white as snow." Isn't that how the words of that old hymn go? Justin was now perfect in heaven, and washed white as snow.

As a dear friend of ours, Mary Woods, said at the age of ninety-nine, "Those who have died haven't gone; they have arrived!"

Somehow I felt left behind, but already God was taking care of me. In fact, He had never stopped caring for me. One of the lines in a Blue Rodeo song called "Five Days in May" says, "He wrote her name in the sand, never even let go of her hand."

Justin was pronounced dead ten minutes after midnight on January 21, only ten days after entering the hospital. But Dan and I have always felt that January 20 was really the day when he passed from this world into the next. He left us before the good doctors and machines could confirm what had already happened.

Months later, I was often tempted to feel guilty for letting the doctors turn those machines off. But God reminded me of the emptiness in that hospital room when I went back one last time, and of His words that prepared us for our son's death. God also reminded me of the words He had given to that woman at our church—that Justin had been crying out in his desire to be with the angels. Dan also told me that Justin's left hand had felt cold before our final meeting with the doctor—a sign that he was beginning to leave us.

And when God told me I was to give the testimony at Justin's funeral, I knew I could trust God; He would enable me to do it. For He had given me a message—"Not in the flesh"—which told me I would not give this public testimony of my son's life in my own strength, but in His strength.

> For we do not preach ourselves, but Christ Jesus the Lord, and ourselves your bondservants for Jesus' sake. For it is the God who commanded light to shine out of darkness, who has shone in our hearts to give the light of the knowledge of the glory of God in the face of Jesus Christ. But we have this treasure in earthen vessels, that the excellence of the power may be of God and not of us. (2 Corinthians 4:5–7, NKJV)

Dan and I chose to place the phrase "at play in the fields of the Lord" on Justin's grave marker, along with an image of grass and wildflowers in memory of the words and image God had given us while he was still in the hospital.

God again reminded me of this word, "field," exactly one year after our son passed away. I looked up this word in my concordance and discovered the verse: *"Let the field be joyful, and all that is in it"* (Psalm 96:12, NKJV). These words brought comfort and assurance to me at a stressful time—the anniversary of Justin's death—as I thought of him running through a green field in his bare toes. Not only was Justin joyful in that field, but all that was in it. Even the flowers were joyful!

> To whom will you liken me and make me equal, and compare me, that we may be alike? (Isaiah 46:5, ESV)

Who can compare to our God?

Who has measured the waters in the hollow
of His hand,
Measured heaven with a span
And calculated the dust of the earth in a
measure?
Weighed the mountains in scales
And the hills in a balance?
Who has directed the Spirit of the Lord,
Or as His counselor has taught Him?

With whom did He take counsel, and who
instructed Him,
And taught Him in the path of justice?
Who taught Him knowledge,
And showed Him the way of
understanding?...

To whom then will you liken God?
Or what likeness will you compare to Him?
The workman molds an image,
The goldsmith overspreads it with gold,
And the silversmith casts silver chains.
Whoever is too impoverished for such a
contribution
Chooses a tree that will not rot;
He seeks for himself a skillful workman
To prepare a carved image that will not
totter.

Have you not known?
Have you not heard?
Has it not been told you from the beginning?
Have you not understood from the
    foundations of the earth?
It is He who sits above the circle of the earth,
And its inhabitants are like grasshoppers,
[We are so many on the earth, and yet God
    knows each of us personally.]
Who stretches out the heavens like a curtain,
And spreads them out like a tent to dwell in.
He brings the princes to nothing;
He makes the judges of the earth useless.

Scarcely shall they be planted,
Scarcely shall they be sown,
Scarcely shall their stock take root in the
    earth,
When He will also blow on them,
And they will wither,
And the whirlwind will take them away
    like stubble.

"To whom then will you liken Me,
Or to whom shall I be equal?" says the
    Holy One.
Lift up your eyes on high,
And see who has created these things,
Who brings out their host by number;
He calls them all by name,

By the greatness of His might
And the strength of His power;
Not one is missing.
(Isaiah 40:12–14, 18–26, NKJV)

Who is this King of glory?
The Lord, strong and mighty,
The Lord, mighty in battle!
(Psalm 24:8, ESV)

Our God had spoken to us, and who was I to argue? He had told us His purpose. I knew I couldn't stand in His way.

I thank God now for telling me to "Leave and go forward." These words were immensely important to me. Without them, I think I would have felt immobilized. I might have been stuck there, standing or kneeling in Justin's hospital room, unable to leave the hospital long after he died! But God knew what I needed. He had given me these words many times, and far enough ahead of time, so that when January 20 came, I was ready. Ready to take one tiny step forward. Every day after that, I had to keep going forward—forward into what God had planned for me.

Don't get me wrong. Going forward wasn't without tears. Feelings of sorrow would inevitably come each day and the tears would flow. But God was there beside me in the pain and encouraged me to grieve.

Jesus says, in Matthew 10:29, that not one sparrow falls without the Father knowing. The sparrow might just be the most plain bird out there! And yet God is concerned about that simple little sparrow. If He is concerned about the tiny sparrow, then surely He is concerned about you, too!

> Are not two sparrows sold for a copper coin? And not one of them falls to the ground apart from your Father's will. But the very hairs of your head are all numbered. Do not fear therefore; you are of more value than many sparrows. (Matthew 10:29–31, NKJV)

Sparrows were considered worthless in the culture in which Jesus lived. Hence the statement was made that two sparrows could be sold for a mere penny. And yet we have much more value than a sparrow, Jesus says. Therefore, we can trust that God knows exactly when you and I struggle and fall. Jesus says, "And not one of them falls to the ground apart from your Father's will." So I know and have peace that my son's death did not occur apart from God's will. Rather, it was His will.

Did you also know that there is a plain little sparrow, called a song sparrow, that has a lovely song? I heard it for the first time at my father's lakeside home while writing this book. This little bird was joyously and confidently singing his song for all to hear. He seemed to know his Heavenly Father loved him and would always provide and care for him.

> Why do you say, O Jacob,
> And speak, O Israel: "My way is hidden from
> the Lord,
> And my just claim is passed over by my God"?

Have you not known? Have you not heard?
The everlasting God, the Lord,
The Creator of the ends of the earth,
Neither faints nor is weary.
His understanding is unsearchable.
He gives power to the weak,
And to those who have no might He increases
    strength.
Even the youths shall faint and be weary,
And the young men shall utterly fall,
But those who wait on the Lord
Shall renew their strength;
They shall mount up with wings like eagles,
They shall run and not be weary,
They shall walk and not faint.
(Isaiah 40:27–31, NKJV)

Many are they who say of me,
"There is no help for him in God." Selah
But You, O Lord, are a shield for me,
My glory and the One who lifts up my head.
I cried to the Lord with my voice,
And He heard me from His holy hill. Selah
I lay down and slept;
I awoke, for the Lord sustained me.
(Psalm 3:2–5, NKJV)

Behold, the eye of the Lord is on those who
    fear him,
on those who hope in his steadfast love,

that he may deliver their soul from death
and keep them alive in famine.
Our soul waits for the Lord;
he is our help and our shield.
For our heart is glad in him,
because we trust in his holy name.
Let your steadfast love, O Lord, be upon us,
even as we hope in you.
(Psalm 33:18–22, ESV)

I know that many of my friends and relatives probably wanted very much for me to move forward after Justin's death. My dad is very relieved and happy that I am at peace and moving forward with my life. However, if he had said to me that he wanted me to move forward shortly after my son's death, I probably would have thought he wasn't being very compassionate in the midst of my grief. Yet this was exactly what God wanted me to do. I am not saying that God's reasons were exactly the same as my earthly father's, but they both wanted the best for me.

The wonderful thing for me was that God was actually able to help me move forward. Our friends and family may want the best for us, but can they actually do this for us, or enable us to change? God, on the other hand, is more than able to empower us and give us the strength to move ahead.

To whom will you liken me and make me equal,
and compare me, that we may be alike? (Isaiah 46:5, ESV)

To everything there is a season,
A time for every purpose under heaven:
A time to be born,
And a time to die;
A time to plant,
And a time to pluck what is planted;
A time to kill,
And a time to heal;
A time to break down,
And a time to build up;
A time to weep,
And a time to laugh;
A time to mourn,
And a time to dance.
(Ecclesiastes 3:1–4, NKJV)

Truly, truly, I say to you, unless a grain of wheat falls into the earth and dies, it remains alone; but if it dies, it bears much fruit. Whoever loves his life loses it, and whoever hates his life in this world will keep it for eternal life. If anyone serves me, he must follow me; and where I am, there will my servant be also. If anyone serves me, the Father will honor him. (John 12:24–26, ESV)

And as He spoke, He no longer looked to them like a lion; but the things that began to happen after that were so great and beautiful that I cannot write them... All their life in this world and all their adventures in Narnia had only been the cover and the title page; now at last they were beginning Chapter One of the GREAT STORY which no one on earth had read; which goes on for ever; in which every chapter is better than the one before.[6]

---

[6] Lewis, C.S. *The Complete Chronicles of Narnia: The Last Battle* (London, U.K.: Harper Collins, 1956), p. 524.

CHAPTER SIX
God Is Patient with Us

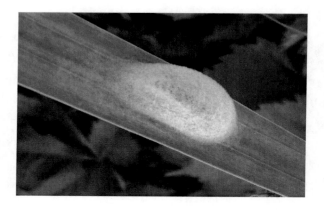

Those who lavish gold from the purse,
and weigh out silver in the scales,
hire a goldsmith, and he makes it into a god;
then they fall down and worship!
They lift it to their shoulders, they carry it,
they set it in its place, and it stands there;
it cannot move from its place.
If one cries to it, it does not answer
or save him from his trouble.

—ISAIAH 46:6–7 (ESV)

But we have this treasure in earthen vessels,
that the excellence of the power may be of
God and not of us.

—2 CORINTHIANS 4:7 (NKJV)

6

As the days since Justin's passing turned into weeks, I found myself struggling with the weight of my emotions. I lamented my son's absence and the total emptiness of our nest. It seemed the reality of his death had finally begun to sink in. One moment I was resting in God's deep peace, and the next I was angry at God for taking my son away.

As this roller coaster of emotions continued, I realized I was afraid to honestly express my anger toward God. I was angry on the inside, but on the outside I refused to really let my emotion show.

You shouldn't get mad at God. Should you?

Even though I knew God was aware of all my thoughts and fears, I still didn't feel comfortable voicing my anger at Him. Others encouraged me to let my emotions out and not keep them bottled up, but still the turmoil continued within me.

Despite all this, God was patient with me. He let me stumble about in my suppressed anger and waited patiently for me to express how I was really feeling.

It took me a long time to fully come through this process. During that time, I learned to feel comfortable saying to God in prayer, "This hurts!" And God's loving response was that He knew and understood my pain.

In time, God helped me to understand the reason for my anger. In my mind, it was one thing to ask God for help, but quite another to tell God that He was wrong. Deep down, I blamed God for my pain. I missed Justin so much and I knew it had been God's decision to have him die at the young age of seventeen.

The anger rose and seemed to rot a hole inside of me until finally, one night, I couldn't stand it any longer. I used my husband as my sounding board. (Poor man! I'm not sure how he put up with me.) I began to yell out everything I had been keeping inside.

As I did this, I realized I was upset at God for telling me to "leave and go forward." How could I? In my mind, this would only bring more pain. I didn't want to leave my son behind. If I continued to "leave and go forward," there would only be more distance between myself and my son, who in my mind was back there on January 21, the day of his passing.

Then finally, when I was silent, God quietly said to me, "Diane, he's ahead of you."

"Oh…" I paused. Then, in the quiet, I finally understood. Each day as I went forward, I wasn't leaving my son further behind; I was moving closer to him. Justin was ahead of me! Finally, my anger was gone and everything made sense.

Some in the church think we must suppress or downplay our anger, anguish, or grief in order to be pious or religious. In the book of Job, Job is in anguish and laments to God that he was ever born:

> After this Job opened his mouth and cursed the
> day of his birth. And Job spoke, and said: "May
> the day perish on which I was born, and the night
> in which it was said, 'A male child is conceived.'"
> (Job 3:1–3, NKJV)

Job's friend, Eliphaz, thinks Job's response is embarrassing, but God does not correct Job for his lament.

As I look back, one of the things that amazes me is how God waited patiently for me to be honest and open with Him. Only after I had released my anger at Him did He respond with His wise and loving response of "Justin is ahead of you."

What can I say? Our God is so very patient with us, and loves us so much. He knew the answer, but He also knew I needed to get my anger out, or it would have rotted my soul.

Our God is so very great! He knows us personally. He knows the core of our pain, and knows just how to heal it. Our God is not just someone we pray and sing to. He is a God who hears us and answers our prayers. He is a God of power and heart! He loves us and fully knows and understands us. He is able to heal and restore our hurts and brokenness. He is the God of all ages, the God of Jacob, and the God of the past, today, and tomorrow.

> Those who lavish gold from the purse,
> and weigh out silver in the scales,
> hire a goldsmith, and he makes it into a god;
> then they fall down and worship!
> They lift it to their shoulders, they carry it,

they set it in its place, and it stands there;
it cannot move from its place.
If one cries to it, it does not answer
or save him from his trouble.
(Isaiah 46:6–7, ESV)

God is not just a figurine on a shelf or a figment of my imagination. I could take gold from my purse, or weigh out silver on the scales, hire a goldsmith, and make it into a god. But could that kind of god wait patiently? Could the kind of god that is made of my imagination wait patiently for me to decide to get angry? Could that god give me healing words at just the right moment and in just the right way to help me personally?

From of old no one has heard or
    perceived by the ear,
No eye has seen a God besides you,
who acts for those who wait for him.
(Isaiah 64:4, ESV)

God is in the business of healing. A woman who had been hemorrhaging for twelve years once approached Jesus, wanting to be healed by Him. Her faith was so great that she said, "If only I may touch His clothes, I shall be made well."

And [Jesus] said to her, "Daughter, your faith has made you well. Go in peace, and be healed of your affliction." (Mark 5:34, NKJV)

From that day forward, her flow of blood was healed. It was her faith that healed her, not any superstition or positive thinking. God is powerful, strong, and helpful. But I can't form Him into the shape or image that I want Him to be. He is who He is already.

God could have rescued me out of my anger weeks before. But He knew I needed to acknowledge my anger before I could be free of it; only then would I be able to truly hear Him.

God is able to take your anger. He can handle it when we yell in His face or pound on His chest. He is a big, strong God, and because He loves us, He encourages us to be honest with Him about our emotions. Pounding on the beach was something my husband once did in anger at God, as a young man. If we bury our emotions, they can cause stress and, ultimately, illness. Healing comes when we are honest with God.

The book of Lamentations is a wonderful example of how the prophet Jeremiah honestly came before the Lord and expressed the *true* feelings of his heart:

> He has besieged me and surrounded me with bitterness and woe. He has set me in dark places like the dead of long ago. (Lamentations 3:5–6, NKJV)

These are not rosy, warm, fuzzy feelings. These are the words of someone in pain, and they are expressed directly to the Lord.

In the verses that follow (Lamentations 3:7–20), Jeremiah cries out his anguish to the Lord, and then in verse 21 his heart turns:

> This I recall to my mind,
> Therefore I have hope.
> Through the Lord's mercies we are not consumed,
> Because His compassions fail not.
> They are new every morning;
> Great is Your faithfulness.
> "The Lord is my portion," says my soul,
> "Therefore I hope in Him!"
> (Lamentations 3:21–24, NKJV)

Jeremiah recognizes the mercy and compassion of his Lord. He realizes they are new every morning. How faithful is our God.

I stand in amazement at God's loving patience. He bends down and scoops me up. He holds me gently when I am hurting and carries me when I can barely stand. He is a loving Father.

> I love the Lord, because He has heard
> My voice and my supplications.
> Because He has inclined His ear to me,
> Therefore I will call upon Him as long as I live.
>
> The pains of death surrounded me,
> And the pangs of Sheol laid hold of me;

I found trouble and sorrow.
Then I called upon the name of the Lord;
"O Lord, I implore You, deliver my soul!"

Gracious is the Lord, and righteous;
Yes, our God is merciful.
The Lord preserves the simple;
I was brought low, and He saved me.
Return to your rest, O my soul,
For the Lord has dealt bountifully with you.

For You have delivered my soul from death,
My eyes from tears,
And my feet from falling.
I will walk before the Lord
In the land of the living.
(Psalm 116:1–9, NKJV)

The Lord builds up Jerusalem; He gathers together the outcasts of Israel. He heals the broken-
hearted and binds up their wounds. He counts the
number of the stars; He calls them all by name.
Great is our Lord, and mighty in power; His understanding is infinite. (Psalm 147:2–5, NKJV)

God is there to help us, not to harm us. He knows what is
best and He has our best in mind.

CHAPTER SEVEN
God Directs Our Path

Remember this and stand firm,
recall it to mind, you transgressors,
remember the former things of old;
for I am God, and there is no other;
I am God, and there is none like me,
                    —ISAIAH 46:8–9 (ESV)

For now the winter is past, the rain is over and gone.
The flowers appear on the earth; the time of singing
    has come.
        —SONG OF SOLOMON 2:11–12 (NRSV)

7

rieving is a process unique to each person, just as each one of us is unique. And yet there are many common elements. My hope is that some of my experiences will provide comfort or wisdom for you in your journey.

Abiding

Grieving is a long and arduous path. Time and time again, during the first six months after Justin's passing, I felt very tempted to think I could speed through the grieving or be done with it altogether. Some days I wanted to vault out of the whole process, skip all the hard days, forget all the memories that brought pain and tears, and leave the dark valley behind.

But God had better plans for me. He wanted me to go through the length and breadth of this process, no matter how difficult it was. Deep down, I knew that was best. I felt God wanted me to be patient, and yet I didn't have it in me to be patient. So I asked friends to pray that I would be willing to stay in what God was doing, whatever that was and for as long as it took. Asking for prayer from friends was tremendously helpful.

But He made His own people go forth
  like sheep,
And guided them in the wilderness like
  a flock;
And He led them on safely, so that they
  did not fear.
(Psalm 78:52–53, NKJV)

However, in order to go forward, even once I knew Justin was ahead of me, I found I needed to rest in God more than I ever had before. I had to learn how to abide in Him and dwell under the shadow of His wings as the waves of grief ebbed and flowed.

Jesus said in John 15:4, *"Abide in Me, and I in you"* (NKJV). "To abide" means to remain, to continue, to dwell, to be present, and to tarry. Like baby chicks safely cuddled under the warm downy feathers of their mother, we can find rest, peace, and healing if we dwell intimately with the Lord. We know our children love to cuddle with us, and they love it  when we slow down and spend intimate time with them. In turn, God loves to dwell intimately with us.

Abiding in the Lord is part of our daily walk with Him. In times of difficulty, it can be especially important. For me, I had to really apply this in the months following our son's death. But we need to remember that this lesson applies to the entirety of our lives, whether we are in the midst of trials or not.

Is it possible to be present with God throughout the day? Can we linger a little longer with the Father each morning, before we head into our daily routine? Where is your dwelling place?

Try to picture yourself in these verses. While you do that, take note of where you place yourself in relation to where God is.

> He who dwells in the secret place of the
> Most High
> Shall abide under the shadow of the
> Almighty.
> I will say of the Lord, "He is my refuge
> and my fortress;
> My God, in Him I will trust."
>
> Surely He shall deliver you from the snare
> of the fowler
> And from the perilous pestilence.
> He shall cover you with His feathers,
> And under His wings you shall take refuge;
> His truth shall be your shield and buckler.
> You shall not be afraid of the terror by night,
> Nor of the arrow that flies by day,
> Nor of the pestilence that walks in darkness,
> Nor of the destruction that lays waste at
> noonday.

A thousand may fall at your side,
And ten thousand at your right hand;
But it shall not come near you.
Only with your eyes shall you look,
And see the reward of the wicked.

Because you have made the Lord, who is
     my refuge,
Even the Most High, your dwelling place,
No evil shall befall you,
Nor shall any plague come near your
     dwelling;
For He shall give His angels charge over you,
To keep you in all your ways.
In their hands they shall bear you up,
Lest you dash your foot against a stone.
You shall tread upon the lion and the cobra,
The young lion and the serpent you shall
     trample underfoot.

"Because he has set his love upon Me,
therefore I will deliver him;
I will set him on high,
because he has known My name.
He shall call upon Me,
and I will answer him;
I will be with him in trouble;
I will deliver him and honor him.

With long life I will satisfy him,
And show him My salvation."
(Psalm 91, NKJV)

The way we each rest in God and spend time with Him is unique. Some do this best in the great outdoors, while others choose a quiet chair at home. I found I needed to take time to absorb my son's death, his absence, and the new shape of my life. As someone said who had lost her sister and her elderly mother and father, all in the course of a few months, "You learn to live a new normal."

What I soon discovered was that my days no longer had any consistency or pattern. So I found that by laying down my old patterns and seeking some kind of direction from God, each day unfolded differently from the next. Sometimes He would bring someone to mind who I should visit with on the phone or in person. Occasionally, He directed me to go somewhere or go on what I would call a "field trip," such as a visit to Justin's school. I found I needed to seek God's direction on multiple occasions throughout the day.

For me the temptation was often to get busy, whereas God's plan was often much quieter and more contemplative. Usually God asked me to lie down, read my Bible, or pray. The pattern of my days became more and more quiet as the weeks and months progressed.

Thankfully, I was blessed to have a husband who supported me in staying home. He understood how important it was to take time to rest, to pray, to talk with God, and to just go for walks with my dog. By spending time alone with God each day, I found that God was able to fill my day, and I found *Him*. And by finding Him, I found peace, healing, and rest.

> Fear not, for I am with you;
> Be not dismayed, for I am your God.
> I will strengthen you,
> Yes, I will help you,
> I will uphold you with My righteous
>   right hand…
>
> I will open rivers in desolate heights,
> And fountains in the midst of the valleys;
> I will make the wilderness a pool of water,
> And the dry land springs of water.
> I will plant in the wilderness the cedar and the
>   acacia tree, the myrtle and the oil tree;
> I will set in the desert the cypress tree
>   and the pine
> And the box tree together,
> That they may see and know,
> And consider and understand together,
> That the hand of the Lord has done this,
> And the Holy One of Israel has created it.
> (Isaiah 41:10, 18–20, NKJV)

I think God wants us to rest in our times of grieving. We don't always want, or know how, to do this. And I know some don't have as much freedom in their schedules to do this as easily as others. But I think this is God's best—His first choice for those of us who are in deep grief—for He knows how important this process is, how intense and tiring it can be, and how long it will take. He created us to love others, and when these loved ones die we grieve their loss deeply. This is normal and healthy, but not easy.

The push to be busy is so prevalent in our culture. I was often asked during the months following Justin's death, "So, are you keeping busy?" But because I knew God wanted me to stay at home and take time to grieve and just be with Him, I found myself telling these well-meaning friends that I was striving for a different B-word: not busy, but balance.

I found that *The Practice of the Presence of God*, by Brother Lawrence,[7] presents one of the best ways to be thoughtfully aware of God on a constant basis. The Holy Spirit never leaves us. What we need to do is become more aware of His presence with us throughout our day. We should set time aside to read the Bible and pray every day. But we also need to remember that God is with us when we are washing the dishes or driving to work. We can talk to Him at these times, too. In fact, we can talk to God throughout our day, whether we are in trouble or not, for He wants to be with us in the good times, too!

Our children can do this as well. Our son loved to have me read the Bible to him or pray with him. But I also know he had conversations with God on a regular basis. I am sure of it! I just can't tell you what they talked about!

Justin also knew what it meant to sit with someone just because he loved being with them. We didn't have to be doing anything; we just sat together. Sure, sometimes we talked

---

[7] Lawrence of the Resurrection, Brother. *The Practice of the Presence of God* (Garden City, NY: Image Books, 1977).

or listened to music, but sometimes we just sat in silence looking out our big picture window in the living room, taking it all in. I think Justin saw the kingdom of God all around him.

Since his passing, God continues to use people like my eighty-year-old father, who in the midst of my busyness said to me just the other day, "Why don't you sit down here?" Dad just wanted me to sit with him. Sometimes we would talk and other times we would just be together in the silence and be at peace with that. When I did stop and be present, I felt such peace and worth in what I was doing (or not doing, as the case may have been). How like our Heavenly Father this is. He just wants to be with us.

> Then little children were brought to Jesus for him to place his hands on them and pray for them. But the disciples rebuked those who brought them. Jesus said, "Let the little children come to me, and do not hinder them, for the kingdom of heaven belongs to such as these." When he had placed His hands on them, he went on from there. (Matthew 19:13–15, NIV)

How I love the wonder of children and their simple adoration of God and His creation. If only we could come to the Father in the same simple way and just adore Him. If only we could just sit down and enjoy being in His presence. This is like Mary, the sister of Martha, who sat at the feet of Jesus rather than rushing to prepare the next meal. This is not to say that household tasks are unimportant, but it does point

out our need to, *"be still, and know that [He is] God"* (Psalm
46:10, NKJV).

Quiet time is something that is often missing in our day-
to-day lives. We run from one task to the next, barely stop-
ping to eat or spend time with those we love. Sadly, a young
teen once told me she didn't feel she had time to spend with
the Lord because she was too busy. We need to find the correct balance between daily needs and spending quality time
with God and the significant people in our lives.

> My help comes from the Lord,
> Who made heaven and earth.
>
> He will not allow your foot to be moved;
> He who keeps you will not slumber.
> Behold, He who keeps Israel
> Shall neither slumber nor sleep.
>
> The Lord is your keeper;
> The Lord is your shade at your right hand.
> The sun shall not strike you by day,
> Nor the moon by night.
>
> The Lord shall preserve you from all evil;
> He shall preserve your soul.
> The Lord shall preserve your going out and
>   your coming in
> From this time forth, and even forevermore.
> (Psalm 121:2–8, NKJV)

Anniversaries

One of the greatest things we can do along our grieving journey is to mark anniversaries. I initially found that I would often think of excuses why I should not do this. But once I had
planned how I would remember that special birthday,
Christmas holiday, or anniversary of my son's death, the
nervousness or fear disappeared and I was able to enjoy the
fact that I had chosen to remember and commemorate that
special person whom I missed so dearly. All the effort was
worth it!

Sometimes I was the one who had to plan the "event," or
else nothing would happen on that special day. But other
times it was God who brought special things into the day or
season. For example, one time God prompted me to buy myself a white cross pendant at the beginning of December that
I had seen months earlier. This was my first Christmas present after Justin died, and I felt it was a present from Jesus to
me. Sometimes we need to be the one to buy that special
present for ourselves. That was just the beginning of many
special little touches that God gave me that Christmas season.

A year later, in early October, I began to think about
Christmas approaching. I am someone who likes to put out
one or two Christmas decorations at a time in my home, and
I like to begin this during the month of October. A day or
two later, I was cleaning out my top dresser drawer and came
across a tiny glass snowman with a colorful scarf and the
name "Justin" printed across its belly. This was a Christmas
ornament I had planned to give him the Christmas he passed
away. It was as if God was applauding my early decorations

and my joy over the coming Christmas season, as I boldly stepped forward without Justin that year. That day we had our first snowfall of the season—another joyful reflection of this little snowman.

Two days later, I realized there was more significance to this little snowman when I received an invitation from the Children's Hospital grief support staff, who were inviting parents who had lost a child due to death, miscarriage, or suicide to a Memory Tree service in which they could place an ornament on a Christmas tree in memory of their child. I joined many other grieving parents that day and placed this tiny snowman on their tree in memory of Justin. God was clearly reaching out, touching me lovingly during the Christmas season, and I realized I didn't need to fear its approach anymore.

How interesting it is that other cultures, from the people of Africa to the Nisga'a Indians on the west coast of Canada, recognize the need to mark the anniversary of a loved one's death. Both of these cultures, on opposite sides of the globe, embrace the fact that their loved ones have impacted their lives deeply and will always be remembered.

My husband's grandparents lost a son at the age of six months. Because their son was sickly and not expected to live, my husband's Granddad chose not to bond with his infant son. However, he lived for six months, and during that time he was lovingly cared for by his mother. Maybe because money was scarce in those days, Granddad chose not to buy a gravestone for the son he scarcely knew. Decades later when her husband died, Grandma went to buy a grave marker for her husband with the help of one of her sons.

When that business was done and her son indicated that it was time to go, she explained that she had another task to fulfill. She had been counting the days, months, and years since the death of her infant son. That day she bought a second grave marker for her son.

Grieving is important. I can't say enough about the importance of marking the anniversaries and birthdays of your friends, family, and pets. My husband's grandmother wanted to celebrate her husband's life by remembering him on his birthday, rather than on the day of his death. When you don't have the opportunity to do this, you miss out. You long to mark that event. By planning ahead, laying down old traditions or expectations, and letting God surprise you, a time of sadness can become one of pure joy!

In time, you will emerge from this long, dark valley into an open vista, green and bright with new life. That day will come if you go forward patiently.

New Life

I discovered a little glimpse of this wide green vista four months after Justin passed away while Dan and I were in Ontario visiting family. As I walked alone through the Columbia Forest in Waterloo, I felt the soft earthen path beneath my feet and looked up at the tall trees around me. Everything was still. Walking along the soft path, I emerged into a beautiful open field that sloped away from me to a quiet farmhouse, a duck pond, and grazing cattle. It was such a peaceful scene that I just had to sit down on the edge of the field and take it all in.

The color of green grass stands for "new life." And that is just what I was beginning to experience on that trip. There was still a great deal of grieving to come after that day, but it was then that I saw a return of joy and had a sense that I could see the sun again.

However, immediately upon experiencing this joy, I sensed a little voice telling me I should feel guilty for feeling joyful, for how could I be joyful when my son was dead? I realized that such a thought could not be from God, for I knew He would not want me to feel guilty for experiencing joy again. So I rejected this thought with a short prayer.

In response to this, I could sense God giving me a message from Justin—"You love me." I felt reassured by these words, which reminded me that my son knew I loved him, and feeling joy again didn't change that. I didn't need to feel guilty.

Justin was someone who loved to show pure, uninhibited joy every day over the simple things in life, like playing his piano or seeing someone he loved walk into the room. So it made perfect sense that he was thrilled that day to see his mom experiencing joy again.

> Weeping may endure for a night, but joy comes
> in the morning. (Psalm 30:5, NKJV)

> For now the winter is past, the rain is over
>   and gone.
> The flowers appear on the earth; the time of
>   singing has come.
> (Song of Solomon, 2:11–12, NRSV)

You have turned my mourning into joyful
    dancing.
You have taken away my clothes of mourning
    and clothed me with joy.
(Psalm 30:11, NLT)

God is amazing! He can bring us up out of darkness and set us upon a bright hill. So when I feel overwhelmed, I try to look back at all He has done to bless and prepare me through this time of our son becoming ill and passing away. By acknowledging and thanking God for what He has done, I find I am lifted once again. In turn, I have a fresh awareness that He is still there to carry me today. Just like the Israelites who needed to remember what their God had done for them, so do we.

Remember this and stand firm,
    recall it to mind, you transgressors,
    remember the former things of old;
    for I am God, and there is no other;
    I am God, and there is none like me,
(Isaiah 46:8–9, ESV)

Isaiah 46:8 says, *"Remember this, and show yourselves men"* (NKJV). I find that these words call me to stand strong as a soldier in the army of God who trusts in her commander-in-chief. We need to stand firm in our faith, knowing that God will take care of the details.

As it says in 1 Corinthians 10:13:

> The temptations in your life are no different from what others experience. And God is faithful. He will not allow the temptation to be more than you can stand. When you are tempted, he will show you a way out so that you can endure. (NLT)

This may seem a harsh statement, but I can now see the truth in it. Even though God allowed Justin to die, which was the hardest thing I have ever gone through, by keeping my eyes upon God I can say that it was not more than I could bear. However, if I had tried to endure it on my own, I am sure I would have crumbled in despair.

> And I said, "This is my anguish;
> But I will remember the years of the right
>   hand of the Most High."
> I will remember the works of the Lord;
> Surely I will remember Your wonders of old.
> I will also meditate on all Your work,
> And talk of Your deeds.
> Your way, O God, is in the sanctuary;
> Who is so great a God as our God?
> You are the God who does wonders;
> You have declared Your strength among the
>   peoples.
> You have with Your arm redeemed Your
>   people,

The sons of Jacob and Joseph.
(Psalm 77:10–15, NKJV)

God is faithful. He chooses the best path for us and then enables us to walk along that path. He doesn't promise to remove all the trials along the way, but He does promise to help us walk through the circumstances of our life when we lean on Him.

"Sometimes He calms the storm, and other times He calms His child."[8]

---

[8] Scott Krippayne. "Sometimes He Calms the Storm" (Wild Imagination, 2002).

CHAPTER EIGHT
God Has a Plan

Declaring the end from the beginning
and from ancient times things not yet done,
saying, "My counsel shall stand,
and I will accomplish all my purpose."
—ISAIAH 46:10 (ESV)

He has made everything beautiful in its time.
He has also set eternity in the hearts of men;
yet they cannot fathom what God has done from
beginning to end.
—ECCLESIASTES 3:11 (NIV)

8

God has a plan for all of us and through the Holy Spirit He has gifted each one of us with many gifts and talents. I believe that if we are seeking to know and follow Him, the Holy Spirit will help us to discover and develop our gifts.

The church is like a body in which each member has a different role to play. The arm has a very different role to play than that of the foot because the arm and the foot are very different in and of themselves. Similarly, a person with the gift of teaching has a different role to play than someone who has the gift of intercessory prayer. Some members of the body may be more prominent or visible, but each plays an equally important role.

I haven't always known what my spiritual gifts are. After having been a Christian for about ten years, God showed me that I had the gift of administration. I, along with two other women, were in charge of planning a ladies' retreat for the women in our church. It was only then that I began to see that planning such an event was something I was good at. The retreat went well, and the women were blessed.

Approximately six years later, in a different church, I again felt a desire to serve the women there by planning a retreat. God had many surprises in store for me throughout the planning process. For example, our speaker, a woman who two of us on the planning committee knew very well, told us that God had already laid a topic on her heart even before we met with her and asked her to be our speaker.

As we moved forward with our plans, we decided that one of us on the planning committee would need to take on a leadership role. I was a bit surprised when God convinced me to take on that position. However, He gave me the peace and organizational skills to do the job. The simple fact that I absolutely loved what I was doing really confirmed for me that administration was one of my spiritual gifts. Phoning, planning, and organizing made me tick!

I have also found that God brings others alongside us who have the same gifts in order to mentor and encourage us as we grow. As I look back, I can see how He did this in the case of each of my spiritual gifts. Today, I am thankful for these gifts in my life. They enable me to grow, to bless others, and to lean more on God.

My gift of teaching was stretched early in my Christian walk when I was given my first opportunity to speak at a girls' Christian summer camp under the direction of a friend. My friend Joyce was to be the main speaker and I was to be her understudy.

But God surprised us and changed our plans. Joyce discovered that she would not be able to speak that summer after all. She was disappointed and apologetic, but surprisingly at peace, too, as she sensed this was something I needed to do on my own—without her, but with God.

When Joyce was no longer able to mentor me and lead in the speaking, I felt God was really taking me out of my comfort zone, which caused me to lean even more on Him. Again, one of my "life verses" came to mind:

> Trust in the Lord with all your heart
> and lean not on your own understanding;
> in all your ways acknowledge him,
> and he will make your paths straight.
> (Proverbs 3:5–6, NIV)

God is more than able to do all that He has begun in your life and mine! He will complete the work He has begun, and His timing is perfect. Only by trusting Him will we have the courage and faith needed to believe that His will and plan are possible.

The great thing about participating in God's plan and purpose for our life is that rather than just going along for the ride, we begin to feel like one of His soldiers, who has a purpose in His army. Through His strength and direction, we begin to work out His purpose in our lives. This can be a very exciting adventure!

It is my desire to follow God's plan for my life. But God's ways are not our ways (Isaiah 55:8). The gifts He gives us are not always what we expect, or what we would even consider within our ability. Sometimes God asks us to do things that are completely outside of our previous experience or comfort zone. He will provide the strength and skills needed to do the job He has given us to do.

> He did not waver at the promise of God through
> unbelief, but was strengthened in faith, giving

glory to God, and being fully convinced that what
He had promised He was also able to perform.
(Romans 4:20–21, NKJV)

If we could do the task without God, we wouldn't need
to rely on Him.

But He said to me, "My grace is sufficient for you,
for my power is made perfect in weakness."
Therefore I will boast all the more gladly about
my weaknesses, so that Christ's power may rest
on me. That is why, for Christ's sake, I delight in
weaknesses, in insults, in hardships, in persecutions, in difficulties. For when I am weak, then I
am strong. (2 Corinthians 12:9–10, NIV)

A New Gift

For a very long time, my husband Dan has had a great desire
to know what God's vision is for him. Two months after
Justin's death, Dan was walking our dog, Jake, in the coulees
near his sister's house in Lethbridge. During that walk, he got
a sense that God was saying that our grieving was a valley
that would eventually open up into a new and widened vista
of opportunity and service. He sensed God saying that this
vista was going to be "a new thing, completely different" for
Diane, but for Dan it was going to be "similar to the past, but
slightly different." He had a fairly good sense as to what
God's vision was for me but didn't want to interfere in what
God was doing. So he kept this to himself. This vision for me

was later confirmed when we visited family in Ontario in May, only two months later.

Throughout that trip, I had a sense that God was revealing His "new life" for me. The color of green grass represents "new life." It was spring and everywhere I looked I saw bright green grass and trees around me. They seemed to be joyfully shouting "new life" to my grieving heart!

While we were in Ontario, Dan and I prayed together, asking God to reveal specifically what His vision was for us.

We spent our last couple of days in Ontario visiting Dan's brother Ian and his wife Lesley. Over dinner, both Ian and Lesley suggested that I should write. What was especially interesting was that they each said this separately and both were surprised when they discovered they had given me the same idea.

At first, I was a bit skeptical about such a role for myself, as I did not consider myself to be a writer at that time. I do journal quite a bit, and I had written a true short story called "The Red Box" a few months earlier. But that was the extent of my writing experience and I didn't see how such a thing would be possible. Dan was also unsure of this, for the same reason. However, it was a part of what he had sensed was included in God's vision for me.

The next day, we had lunch with Ian and again he said that I should consider writing. Rather than dismissing his comment this time, I decided to embrace the possibility. I felt that if this was something from God, He would make that clear. As we left later that afternoon for the Waterloo airport and our flight home to Calgary, I thanked them for their encouragement.

About thirty minutes later, as I sat in the passenger seat of our car watching the scenery pass by, I felt God telling me to write in my journal. This surprised me, as I didn't think I had anything to write. But I took out my journal and opened it on my lap.

"Justin outline" were the words God gave me. So I wrote these words on the top of my page. For the next half-hour, God proceeded to give me the entire outline for this book, which I wrote in point form in my journal. It was now obvious to me that God was making His vision for me very clear and that I needed to accept that He was asking me to write.

I realize now that God takes His time in revealing His plan to us. He does this gradually and in His time. Looking back, I recall more than one person suggesting that I write a book about Justin. The Bible says,

> Humble yourselves, therefore, under the mighty hand of God so that at the proper time he may exalt you, casting all your anxieties on him, because he cares for you. (1 Peter 5:6–7, ESV)

God is accomplishing all His purposes in and through us.

> Declaring the end from the beginning
> and from ancient times things not yet done,
> saying, "My counsel shall stand,
> and I will accomplish all my purpose."
> (Isaiah 46:10, ESV)

I, for one, want to be a part of what God is doing. I believe it was Helen Keller who once said, "When one door of happiness closes, another opens; but often we look so long at the closed door that we do not see the one which has been opened for us."

There were times when the depth of my grief could have kept me from following God's plan for my life. He had a new vista, a new life, in mind for me. Sometimes the depth of my grief still threatens to keep me from writing because the grief is draining, and some days I don't feel I have the strength to go on.

> "For I know the plans I have for you," declares the Lord, "plans to prosper you and not to harm you, plans to give you hope and a future." (Jeremiah 29:11, NIV)

God is faithful. He will give us the strength and all we need to fulfill His plan for our lives. We need to trust Him and be willing to sacrifice our comfort for His will. This will not always be easy or glamorous, but rather just plain hard work. His rewards are everlasting!

A Symbol

In June 2009, while attending a ladies' retreat at Thetis Island Capernwray Bible School on the West Coast, a particular tree caught my attention while I was walking alone in the woods. I walked beneath it and looked up into its large canopy. Its

leaves were the size of my hand and stretched high above
me.

At first I was stunned and amazed by its beauty. The sun
shone through its big, beautiful leaves. It was such a glorious
tree—tall and majestic. My life seemed to be pictured in this
tree.

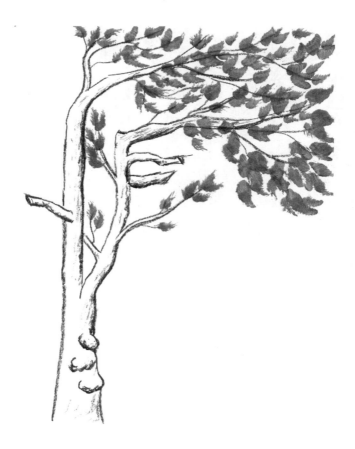

I noticed that near the bottom of the trunk there were
several large "sick-looking" bumps. Above these bumps, the
trunk split into two.

The left trunk was bare of branches and leaves except at the top, where it had a mighty and beautiful canopy. This trunk was tall and straight. Partway up, there was one dead branch jutting outward that had been snapped off.

The other trunk, on the right, had a few leafy branches here and there on the way up. This right trunk continued straight for a long ways, and then *wham*, there was a radical change! Two sharp, ugly, dead branches, jutting outward, had been ripped off the main trunk. At this point, the right trunk took a sharp turn to the right and grew upward and outward with an abundance of leaves, producing a beautiful canopy beneath the leaves of the other trunk on the left.

Interpretation

Just as the sun shone through this tree's beautiful canopy of leaves, so does the Son of God shine through my life. The large, sick-looking bumps at the bottom of the tree reminded me of the horrible dating experiences I had in my early life, and my divorce years later. Just above these bumps, the trunk split into two, signifying how five years later I was no longer alone, but joined in marriage to Dan.

The left trunk seemed to represent Dan's life. It was bare of branches and leaves except at the top, symbolizing the tremendous spiritual growth and fruitfulness that occurred in his later life. This trunk was tall and straight, like Dan's straightforward devotion to God and the church. Partway up, there was one dead branch, jutting outward, that had been snapped off, representing the painful separation that occurred in Dan's life when Justin died.

The trunk on the right represented my life. The few leafy branches here and there on the way up represented the beginnings of spiritual growth and fruitfulness in my early life, nurtured through mentoring and Bible studies.

This trunk continued straight for a long way, and then suddenly there were two sharp, ugly, dead branches, jutting outward, that had been ripped off the main trunk, just as Michael and Justin had been ripped from my arms.

At this point, the right trunk took a sharp turn to the right and grew upward and outward with an abundance of leaves. This represented the new life which followed the death of my son, and how God helped me to develop new skills which yielded fruitfulness, touching many others.

My leafy canopy grew under the protective shelter of that of my mate, Dan, who stands tall and strong beside me. He has been a wonderful protector in my life. I am grateful for God's provision through Dan's skills and job, which has enabled me to stay at home and write. My gifts have been able to flourish under his care and encouragement. I am thankful for his leadership in our home.

CHAPTER NINE
God Loves Us

Listen to me, you stubborn of heart,
you who are far from righteousness.
—ISAIAH 46:12 (ESV)

No man has power over the wind to contain it;
so no one has power over the day of his death.
—ECCLESIASTES 8:8 (NIV)

9

The butterfly theme began in my life in 2007 when I received the gift of a Josh Groban CD from my good friend, Mary Lou. She insisted I listen to the song titled "Lullaby," saying that this song was meant especially for me.

She was right; this song spoke to my heart. The phrase "Rest your wings, my butterfly" seemed to speak of my first child whom I had lost in miscarriage nineteen years before. The words were expressions of my loss, the pain, my love, and the need to release this child. I listened to this lullaby again and again with tears in my eyes.

Miscarriage can often be a death that is not grieved. This's how it was for me for nine years. It was only during the past ten years that I finally began to grieve the loss of my first child, Michael.

The phrase "my butterfly" seemed to fit perfectly, as I know one should not hold a butterfly captive. It must be released—free to fly! I knew I needed to be more at peace with Michael's freedom in heaven and not try to keep him here with me. I needed to surrender my child again into the arms of God. This was difficult, but through prayer I was able to release Michael.

A year later, in January 2008, when Justin became seriously ill and God told my husband and me that he might not make it through his illness, this song began to come to my mind again. This time I pictured Justin as I listened to the words of this beautiful lullaby. As I drove back and forth to the hospital, I listened to the song again and again and began to think about how I would need to release our second little butterfly into the hands of the Lord and heaven's grasp.

That week, while Justin lay in the ICU, a second butterfly incident occurred. Dan and I needed to return to our car, which was parked in the hospital parkade. On our way there, we passed by the pay booth which was enclosed in glass. These glass windows were decorated with many, many large, brightly-colored pictures of butterflies!

I went up to the attendant behind the glass and said, "This is going to sound odd, but when did you put these butterflies up?"

"A couple of days ago," the attendant replied, which meant the butterflies had been put up around the time Justin went into the ICU.

Later, as I drove to and from the hospital, I knew God was prompting me with details of what should be included in Justin's funeral service. I knew that I wanted Josh Groban's "Lullaby" to be part of the service. In the meantime, God continued to give me peace about where He was taking Justin.

As I stood by my son's hospital bed later that week, with a wet Kleenex in my hand, I thrust my arms in the air and my little ball of Kleenex shot up and out of my hand. I was releasing my little butterfly into God's hands.

On Monday, January 21, 2008, only days later, Justin entered the embrace of our Lord and was joyfully greeted by many angels. Our second little butterfly had entered heaven. However, the butterfly theme that would become a part of my life had only just begun!

A few months later, Kasia, another good friend of mine, excitedly told me she had something to tell me about butterflies—something God wanted her to share with me. I was stunned, as I hadn't told Kasia any of my butterfly stories yet. She went on to describe the different stages of the butterfly to me, and as she did I began to understand that this symbol of the butterfly represented Justin's *entire* precious life, his illness, and his release into heaven.

I saw that the caterpillar stage represented his time here on earth, a time when he could move around, but he was limited to what his wheelchair or walker enabled him to do. Justin had started life in a body that was somewhat restricted in its movements. He always needed to be patient and willing to depend upon others and the equipment provided for him.

The caterpillar, or larval stage, is also a stage of incredible growth. In order to accommodate this, the caterpillar must eat, and eat! Oh, how my son loved to eat, especially bananas and desserts!

When Justin was in the ICU, his health was critical. The fluid from his severe sinusitis and pneumonia was causing his lungs to collapse. He had to be placed on a special oscillating respirator, which did his breathing for him. This respirator did not use a regular breathing pattern. All of his muscles needed to be paralyzed with a drug so that he would not breathe against the pattern of the respirator. Justin also had many tubes—some into his veins and others down his throat. The paralyzing drug also kept our son perfectly still and unable to pull out any of these important tubes.

Justin really was in a cocoon—a cocoon in which he could not move even the tiniest little muscle, not even his eyelids. This is just like the pupa stage, for it is known that when caterpillars go into their cocoon, or pupa stage, they are inactive and usually sessile (unable to move).

Justin was released from the cocoon of his hospital bed in time for heaven's gates to be opened wide for him. In His time, God had placed our son in heaven as His servant. This servant was gone from his mother's arms and was now free from his hospital cocoon! In heaven, no restrictions, such as wheelchairs and walkers, could prevent him from moving about in total, blissful freedom! Just as a caterpillar undergoes a complete metamorphosis, so did Justin, for his body is no longer handicapped, but strong and tall.

God understands a mother's pain in losing her child, for He allowed His Son to leave His side and come down to Earth two thousand years ago. Thirty-three years later, God chose to allow His Son to die on the cross as payment for our sins. While Jesus hung on that cross, Father and Son were separated, a torturous separation, a tearing apart of what had always been One.

I, too, experienced a feeling of tearing, as though a limb had been torn from my body, a limb that had been there for eighteen years. God had sacrificed His only Son. Now I had to release my only remaining son. God's Son was His best treasure! Justin, too, was my best treasure, and I found it extremely hard to truly let him go, even months after his death.

Five months after he passed away, I began to experience inner tension as his birthday approached and I anticipated the difficult grieving this day would bring. I prayed and asked God to direct how we could make this first birthday without Justin a special day.

About two weeks before his birthday, I received a phone call from Justin's schoolteacher. She wanted to invite me to a birthday celebration in memory of our son! She said that Justin's classmates had been raising butterflies in the classroom and they wanted to release them on his birthday! I was stunned. She could not have known the meaning that butterflies now held for me! I could only repeatedly stammer "Wow!" into the phone as we made plans for me to come to the school on June 18. I could see that Justin's birthday would truly be a special day! (We later learned from one of the aides in his classroom that God had prompted her to tell the other classroom staff they should raise butterflies and release them on Justin's birthday.) God was continuing to use the symbol of the butterfly.

As June 18 approached, I continued to experience intense inner tension that I didn't fully understand. One night, I asked Dan about a prayer he had prayed with Justin while he lay sick in the hospital, unable to move. That had been the day when his blood pressure had been extremely low. The nurses had been very concerned and had called in Justin's doctor, who tried to adjust his medication. But nothing seemed to help. So the medical people were forced to simply watch and monitor him. This was especially hard on his nurse that day. This concerned me as well, and I began to sense that Justin was worried about something, causing his blood pressure to drop. So I approached his bedside and stood quietly at his left side. Justin was still unable to move or speak due to the paralyzing drug, but we could rely on the Holy Spirit to help us. Ever since Justin had become a believer, I had depended upon the Holy Spirit to give me insight into what Justin wanted to say to me but couldn't due to his disability and limited speech.

"Hurt," was the first word I received through the Holy Spirit.

"Who's hurt?" I asked aloud.

"You," was the reply.

"Do you think Mom is hurt?" I asked Justin.

"Yes."

"Do you think Justin being sick hurts Mom?" I asked, wording my question as simply as I could.

"Yes. Sorry."

"But it was not Justin's idea to get sick," I said quickly to him, not wanting my son to blame himself. "This was God's idea. Mom will be okay. God will help Mom."

At this point, I noticed that his blood pressure was normalizing. This was exciting to see, as I dearly wanted to help Justin. Trying to be helpful, and not wanting my son to cope with this illness in his own strength, I told him that he needed to rest in God and let Him do it. Immediately I was given the word "anger." I knew Justin was angry, and in perfect concert with this response was a drop in his blood pressure again.

His nurse came striding into his room and said, "I think you need to stop talking to him!" I agreed. There was nothing I could do to change Justin's mind. I knew this was between him and God. I went back to my reclining chair a few feet away.

A while later, Dan arrived in the ICU. I told him what had transpired and asked him to pray with Justin. I sensed I should not interfere, but let Dan pray alone with him. While he prayed, I watched the blood pressure gauge and Justin's blood pressure go from abnormally low back to normal. Justin was relaxed and at peace after that. He must have surrendered his fears and worries into God's hands that night.

Two days later, God gave Dan the phrase "at play in the fields of the Lord," and I was given a picture of green grass. Three days later, we said goodbye to our son and left the hospital knowing he was now bounding happily through grassy fields of flowers in heaven in his bare toes. No more restrictions or disabilities. He was truly free.

Four and a half months later, grieving heavily from the loss of our son, I asked Dan what he had prayed with Justin that day. Dan replied, "I prayed that God would give Justin peace. I told him that if God was calling him, that Mom and 'Da' would be okay. I told him that it was up to him whether he stayed here with us or went to be with God. If he decided to go to God, Mom and 'Da' would be okay. We would miss him, but we would be okay. If he decided to stay here with us, we would take care of him and we would be happy to have him here with us. But if God was calling him, it would be best to listen to God, for He knows best."

That night was a difficult one for me. I found myself still rebelling against what God was doing. Justin's eighteenth birthday was only days away. How could we celebrate it without Justin? I wanted my son with me.

But he wasn't just my son. First and foremost, Justin belonged to God, for it was God who made him. In the story of Punchinello, in Max Lucado's book *You Are Special*, Eli the woodcarver tells little Punchinello, "I made you."[9] Punchinello, like Justin, is God's child, and I needed to remember that he had only been loaned to me for a time.

I sensed that God was telling me to release Justin again. My son was already in heaven and had been there for four and a half months. But oh, this was hard! I struggled against God's will—unsuccessfully, of course! I was like a little child struggling against her very strong but loving Father. The words God gave me that night were "Give" and "Release." So again, I released my son into my Father's hands; he was safe there.

A few days later, I began to understand more deeply what God was doing. This upcoming butterfly release at Justin's school was beginning to take on a new and deeper meaning. God had clearly orchestrated this whole thing, for only He could have brought together all these butterfly events, one after the other. Who else could have told Justin's classroom aide that they needed to raise butterflies in memory of my son on his birthday? It was clearly His plan. God meant the gift of the butterfly for me! He had woven all these details together: first through the Josh Groban song, then through the butterflies on the window in the parkade, followed by my friend who explained the stages of the butterfly, and now through the releasing of real butterflies on Justin's birthday. How amazing! All of this love—God's love—was for me!

---

[9] Lucado, Max. *You Are Special* (Wheaton, IL: Crossway Books, 1997), p. 23.

Have you ever stopped and *fully* accepted the fact that the God of the universe really loves you? Have you, like me, maybe never really fully accepted that? Are you just too broken and imperfect in your own eyes for Him to really love you? Or maybe, like me, you are a bit of a stubborn rebel. God spoke through the prophet Isaiah, saying:

> Listen to me, you stubborn of heart,
> you who are far from righteousness:
> (Isaiah 46:12, ESV)

God did a wonderful thing when He sent His Son, Jesus, to die for us. His death was enough; He didn't need to do anything more. Yet every day He gives us these little living touches that reach out to us. We need only keep our eyes open for these "little butterflies" that speak to us of His amazing love.

A few days later, I excitedly told another friend about Justin's upcoming birthday party at the school. Marilyn was a longtime friend who had always said our children are not our own; they belong to God. However, when she told me this in the past, I must admit I had only agreed with her intellectually, for at that time I had never been asked to completely give my child over into God's hands. Justin had always been mine to care for, and mine to love. I knew God loved him, but I was his mother! Now so much had changed and Justin was in heaven. I truly understood what it meant to release my son into God's hands and accept that my son belonged to Him.

Marilyn, too, was beginning to understand more fully this concept of our children not being our own, as she was in the process of moving her eighteen-year-old handicapped daughter into a group home.

As we talked, a yellow butterfly fluttered to and fro through the field beside my parked van, and then right past my window. It was as if God and Justin were shouting their approval as Marilyn and I talked excitedly about what God was doing and about the peace I finally felt about this anniversary.

The next day was Justin's birthday, a day of celebration! I wanted so much to share with everyone there how much the symbol of the butterfly meant to me. Friends and family came to the school and we all shared in the joyous occasion. There were tears as we all attended a music therapy class with Justin's classmates, especially as one of them hugged me, which reminded me so much of my son. After being presented with a very special gift of music from the students and teachers, we went outside for the butterfly release.

It was a warm day and we gathered near the front door of the school, where shrubs would provide a safe place for the butterflies to land. About twenty-one orange butterflies were safely held in a large netted container and I was invited to be the first to release one of them.

Releasing butterflies was not what I had expected, for it is nothing like releasing balloons into the air all at once. These little creatures were very content to stay in their netted home. It was our job to reach into the container and gently place our finger against their tiny feet. Only then would they step onto our hand so we could bring them out into the bigger world.

The butterfly in my hand was in no hurry to leave. It seemed content to just sit there with its beautiful orange and black wings outstretched upon the palm of my hand. So I chose to take that moment to share all the amazing stories about butterflies and the meaning of this wonderful symbol for me. Just as I finished speaking, the butterfly on my hand took flight. Everyone gasped! God's timing had been perfect!

One by one, everyone had the opportunity to carefully lift out a butterfly. It seemed there was a gentle message in these tiny creatures that chose to rest a while upon the hand of each one there that day. In turn, the butterflies elicited a response of pure joy and contentment from the handicapped children in Justin's class and the visitors who had come to join them. The day was very special!

For me, the message of the day continued to be one of God's love for everyone there, and so very much for me, as Justin's mother. God understood our grief and was responding with pure love. As it says in Ephesians 3:18,

> And may you have the power to understand, as all God's people should, how wide, how long, how high, and how deep his love really is. (NLT)

Two months later, another chapter of the butterfly theme occurred in our lives. I was out for lunch with Marilyn and Mary Lou (who had given me the Josh Groban CD). I excitedly told them about all the amazing things God had been doing with butterflies in my life. They were amazed!

Marilyn responded by saying that she wanted to buy me a little figurine of an angel holding a butterfly. I was impressed by her kindness but didn't realize just how special this would become.

Marilyn sought to buy this gift for me, but she could not find it in any store. One day she was shopping with her friend, Lorna, and they asked the store clerk to look up this particular figurine in their catalogue. But it wasn't there.

Lorna interjected, saying, "Marilyn, I have that same statue at home. I would love to give it to Diane."

"Oh no!" Marilyn replied. "That's yours! It was a gift from someone and probably has special meaning for you."

Lorna later realized that Marilyn was right, and this prompted Marilyn to look again for the statue in a gift shop, where she immediately found one.

How incredible all of this was! Marilyn had a desire to give me this little figurine, and yet, even though she couldn't find one in the stores initially, God was able to use that situation to introduce me to Lorna. So I received this beautiful gift of an angel holding out a butterfly. The angel's hands were open, ready to release this butterfly to freedom, just as I had released my son into freedom when he was ill and dying.

Months later, as Justin's next birthday (his nineteenth) approached, I realized that again I wanted to celebrate this day in a special manner. The previous year the school had planned the celebration, but this year I knew I would have to plan it. When I stopped to think of what I wanted to do, the idea of hang-gliding came to my mind—not alone, but doubling with someone.

At first I was a bit unsure if I should do something so crazy and frivolous! However, Dan encouraged me to go ahead with my plans. So, after many delays and thoughts of giving up, I finally connected with a fellow who teaches hang-gliding and other outdoor adventure sports like para-gliding, kayaking, and mountain climbing.

When my family found out what I was planning, they were very surprised. My dad phoned me, curious about what I was doing. He wanted to go hang-gliding, too! My niece, Stephanie, also wanted to join us. The celebration was beginning to take shape!

We were fortunate to be able to do this the day immediately preceding Justin's birthday. As we drove to the site east of Calgary, I explained to my niece and father how the hang-gliding reflected the butterfly and the need to release Justin when we knew he was dying in the hospital. The hang-gliding also reminded us of our son's joy and his love of going fast.

Doubling on a hang-glider can be done in two ways—the first is in the mountains, launching off a cliff; the second is

being pulled behind a pick-up truck, which then releases you into the air. Our pilot and teacher chose the latter method for us. The hang-glider was attached to the tailgate of the truck, which had a winch in the back and a very long tow rope (along with a lot of other technical equipment). The two riders were to get into separate harnesses, which were suspended from the glider. I rode beside and slightly above the fellow who piloted the glider.

Our takeoff consisted of the truck driving very quickly about fifty meters down a narrow country road. At that point our pilot released us, which allowed the glider to pop up about seventy feet into the air! Whoosh! We gently and steadily climbed higher and higher while the truck barreled down the dirt road, pulling us with an ever-increasing length of tow rope.

After the truck pulled us about three miles down the road, we released the tow rope, which dropped gently back down to the ground suspended by a tiny kite. We had an amazing view of the countryside and the Rocky Mountains to the west. In fact, I got up to 2100 feet! How I loved the quiet, gentle ride we had that day over the prairies.

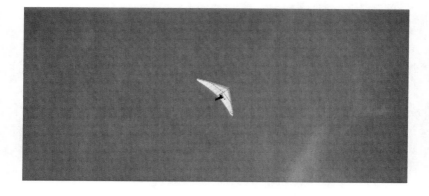

I learned two lessons that day. One was to look back and remember the lessons God had taught me through the symbol of the butterfly. The other was to release my life into God's hands. The fellow who piloted the glider had said, "Every trip is different. You never know which way you'll go or for how long." The trip is totally dependent upon the wind, over which we have no control. Just like our lives, in which every day we spend in relationship with God is a new adventure, you never know which way He'll take you or how long it will be before He turns you in a new direction. But God is in control. He is our pilot, and it is the Holy Spirit who fills our "sails" with wind.

As I watched the others take their turn hang-gliding, I knew it was time for me to release my life more completely into His hands. As I wrote these words into my journal, a tiny white butterfly flew by!

Butterflies continue to encourage me today, especially when I am discouraged or missing my son. Another butterfly incident happened just after Justin's nineteenth birthday and our hang-gliding celebration. We had invited another niece to spend two weeks of holidays with us. However, I found her trip brought on memories of our holidays with Justin over the years. Tearfully, I realized that I missed his happy presence in our family and his joy when travelling.

As the three of us walked along the river near our home, Dan discovered a large beautiful butterfly with black wings tipped with red and yellow. It was underfoot, sunning itself on the beach path. I knelt down and Dan encouraged me to pick it up. I gently placed my finger against its feet, remembering how this had worked so well on the day of the butterfly release at Justin's school. The butterfly calmly stepped onto my finger and I was able to slowly stand while holding the butterfly. Dan then prompted me to tell our niece the story of the butterfly, and as I finished speaking the butterfly left my hand and lazily flew away.

The message is that we need to release things into God's hands, and we need to know and truly accept that God loves us!

God again showed me this same lesson through my friend, Kasia, who had earlier taught me to examine the stages of the butterfly's life. She gave me a butterfly pendant which had come from her homeland of Poland. She fully understood the significance of the butterfly in my life and was thrilled to find a pendant made of amber—the golden brown resin of evergreen trees. How appropriate—for Jesus Christ died on a wooden cross, and the evergreen tree of *Christ*mas time reminds us of how he died on a tree.

As Christmas approached, two years after Justin's passing, I lost this very special butterfly pendant and my favorite silver chain. As my initial attempts to find the necklace at home and in my car failed, I realized how hard this task had become. After silently praying and listening to God, I remembered that I had gone to the secondhand store that day. I quickly phoned them and was told that they had my silver chain, but not the pendant.

As I drove to the secondhand store, I realized what an incredible miracle it would be to find this pendant, for it could have fallen down while I was on the street. In the store or on the street, anyone could have picked it up! I had to surrender the situation completely into God's hands. I knew that in the big scheme of things this was a relatively small loss. And yet I knew that God loves us and cares about the little details of our lives.

When I spoke to the clerk, she said they had looked for the pendant after I phoned, but it was nowhere to be found. She also told me that they vacuumed every night, so it couldn't be on the floor. As she said this, a quick thought flashed through my mind—the vacuum bag! And yet, I knew I would need God's help if I was to look there!

Immediately, this clerk asked me if I wanted to look in the vacuum bag. Stunned, I quickly agreed. She insisted that I take the bag out of the store to do this, nervous about how this might appear to others. I understood and took the bag out to my car, where I gently ripped it open—and there was my butterfly pendant!

God had performed a little miracle—just for me—again! I realized that releasing the situation into His hands had been the right thing to do. In turn, I could see God's love for me, and how He desires to bless me.

Oh, how He loves us!

"He wants us to fall in love with Him, because He is in love with us. It's that simple, and it's that profound."[10]

---

[10] Jackson, John Paul. *7 Days Behind the Veil"* John Paul Jackson, (Texas, U.S.A.: Streams Publishing House, 2008), pp. 30–31.

CHAPTER TEN
God Is Driving

Calling a bird of prey from the east,
the man of my counsel from a far country.
I have spoken, and I will bring it to pass;
I have purposed, and I will do it.

—ISAIAH 46:11 (ESV)

Trust in the Lord with all your heart
and lean not on your own understanding;
in all your ways acknowledge him,
and he will make your paths straight.

—PROVERBS 3:5–6 (NIV)

10

The Trust Game is a game Dan played at the camp where he and I first met; it teaches you about trust. Each person has a partner; one person leads and the other is blindfolded. I invite you to imagine yourself in this situation, blindfolded and dependant upon your partner to protect you from a myriad of obstacles, such as a tree root along the ground, a narrow footbridge, or a muddy swamp. Now imagine there are ten other partners along the same path at the same time. You will need to focus on your partner's voice amongst all the other voices, and you will need to relinquish control of your situation into the hands of someone else, trusting them fully and following their guidance. Life is like that game. The question is: who or what is in control of your life? And whose voice are you listening to?

Wanting to be in charge of my own life has always been a big issue for me. Time and time again, this has created significant problems in my marriage as I try to direct things in a way that serves my purposes rather than thinking of my husband's needs. Releasing my life more completely into God's hands has been a gradual process. I know that His ways are not our ways and that He is all-knowing and wants the best for me. Yet I often hesitate to let Him direct all, not just some, of the details of my life.

The wonderful thing is that God has continued to encourage me every step of the way. He is my loving Father who never gives up on me and patiently teaches me to trust Him more and more each day.

An example of this occurred when I surrendered something into my husband's hands that I had been directing for several years. When Dan and I married, I had already been on my own for five years and was comfortably managing my financial affairs. Dan brought many strengths to the marriage, including a great deal of experience in the area of accounting. However, he was not careful with his spending and had accumulated some debt. This caused me to take control of our expenses, and as a result I became very cautious.

A few years later, God told me to surrender this area into Dan's hands. God was asking me to trust Him and to trust my husband. This was very hard for me initially. But as I listened to God and accepted His words of encouragement, I began to see that God was right! Dan was now managing our finances wisely, and was becoming very thoughtful in his decision-making, especially with regards to our savings and donations.

After years of practicing this attitude of surrender, I have found that my fear of losing control over this area of my life has disappeared, and I have been able to put all our money matters into the hands of my husband. By obeying God, I have put my faith in Him and demonstrated that I trust Dan to lead in this area. This has caused him to feel respected and has eliminated a great deal of disagreements and stress, freeing me to focus on other things.

In turn, God has rewarded us with an ample income which has enabled us to bless others who are in need. Dan has always had the gift of giving, but now God is challenging him to share even more of what He has given us. It is God who provides. Sometimes He asks us to share His provision with others. As we do this, Dan and I are learning to give more willingly, while others are being challenged to receive a gift. We are all part of one body, using our gifts to bless one another. We need to be ready to receive what God has called someone else to give.

In addition, I am learning the tremendous layers of blessing that can occur when you trust and obey the Lord. Rather than leaning on my own understanding, I am realizing that God's knowledge of the situation is much deeper and more complete than what I can see from my superficial and somewhat selfish point of view.

Those who are unfamiliar with the ways of God might find this approach to life rather unusual, for our culture teaches us to be independent and self-directed. But God asks us to lean on Him. As it says in Psalm 118:8, *"It is better to take refuge in the Lord than to trust in man"* (NIV).

Our culture teaches us that we should be in control of our lives and that it is better to have things "our way." However, God's ways are not like those of the world. Jesus said that in the kingdom of God the last shall be first and the first shall be last (Mark 9:35). How different that is! Jesus also surprised His disciples when He, as their master and teacher, bent down as a servant and washed their feet (John 13:1–17). Christianity goes against the grain of our culture and causes us to rethink the way we live. The Bible also says, *"Trust in*

the Lord with all your heart and lean not on your own understand-
ing; in all your ways acknowledge him, and he will make your
paths straight" (Proverbs 3:5–6, NIV).

Let me illustrate this further by telling you about a dream
I had about six years after Dan and I were married. First, we
need to remember that God would never convey something
through a dream that contradicts what the Bible teaches. The
Bible is the main way that He communicates with us; it is
important to respect the authority of God's Word and know
that it supersedes all other ways of hearing from Him. When
evaluating a dream, Scripture should be our guide, or "meas-
uring stick," to help us to decide whether something is from
God or not.

In this dream, I was sitting in the back seat of a car with a
chocolate bar in my hand, feeling very frustrated with the
driver because he was traveling in the left-hand lane of a very
busy road. I was not comfortable with the fact that I had no
control over how he was driving. It seemed that I wanted to
be in control so that I could feel safe and have things my way.

When Dan and I discussed the dream the next morning,
we realized that the driver of the car in my dream had to be
Dan, as he often drove in the left-hand lane, a habit which
always frustrated me. I had been born and raised in British
Columbia, where you are required to stay in the right-hand
lane of a highway unless you are passing another car. My
husband, on the other hand, was born in California and spent
his school years in Ontario, where freeways abound and you
can travel and pass in either lane.

This dream helped me to see I was spending too much of
my energy being angry or frustrated with the lack of control I

had in my marriage. I needed to just relax and let Dan lead, and enjoy the ride—and eat my chocolate bar! What a picture!

God used the image of a car again while Justin was ill in the hospital. This was shortly after God had told Dan and me that Justin "might not make it." This time, Dan was given the image. He saw himself standing on a sidewalk while he watched a car go by. Our son was in the back seat and God was driving. Dan clearly felt God was telling him not to interfere in what He was doing because He was in control, and neither Dan nor I would have any say in what He was doing with regards to Justin's illness. As God says in Isaiah 46:11, *"I have spoken, and I will bring it to pass; I have purposed, and I will do it"* (ESV).

God had a plan for our family, and for Justin. He had spoken to us and nothing we could do would stop what He was doing. We needed to accept His will and be at peace with the fact that our Father was in the driver's seat and was bringing about His good purposes for our lives. Just like in the Trust Game, we wanted to ensure that we continued to listen to *God's* voice and follow *His* plan for our lives.

God knows what is best for us and we need to let Him be Lord of our life. This means we need to let Him drive. Sometimes this can be scary, especially when we would rather be the one driving and know where He is taking us. This isn't always the way God works. Sometimes He gives us a glimpse of where we are going. But often He just asks us to trust Him without knowing our destination.

God is taking us home. Often we cannot see the way ahead, like riding in the back seat and letting someone else drive. We can trust that He is driving and knows the way. The journey ahead could be rocky or smooth, and our path might be long or short, and yet our great comfort is in knowing that we don't need to know all the details of the trip. It is like visiting friends or relatives for the first time in a big city. If they are leading, we don't need to know where we are going next because we trust them to know the way. This is how it is with God. He has our path planned; we are just pilgrims on a journey. We can trust that God knows the way to heaven and eternity. As it says in John 14:6, Jesus is *the* way, *the* truth, and *the* life (my paraphrase).

Remember that God has a plan in mind for your life. He made you just the way you are, and He knows you even better than you do. He has given you gifts and talents that will enable you to serve the body of Christ, the church. Sometimes the plan God has in mind for you is not what you might expect; He may have a surprise in mind for you, and even now He is weaving all the details together.

God used my son to shape me and mold me into the person I am today. Justin was an instrument in God's hand, teaching me and many others to love, to live joyfully, and to accept others without judgment. Once God had taken him to heaven, I had to accept a different path for my life and I needed to let God steer me in the right direction. Certainly, it was not easy to accept the fact that God was taking my son away, nor was it easy to look forward when I didn't have any idea what the future would look like. All I knew was that I needed to follow God and let Him drive, for He knows the way. I do not. Only then could I receive God's best—*His* plan for my life.

A good example of our relationship with God is one of a master and his dog. Most dogs are like mine in that if I choose to take a brand new route for our walk, he will be surprised and wonder where we are going. My dog finds this situation challenging. He knows he needs to continue to walk close to my side, but at the same time he is wondering where we are going. When Justin died, I had no idea where we were going other than out that hospital door. What I did know was that all I wanted to do was stay close to God's side, for I couldn't possibly lead in such a situation. I had to stay close to my Master and loving Father, for only He knew what was around the next corner.

Today my life looks very different from when I was the mother and full-time caregiver of a handicapped child. So much change can be rather daunting, and even frightening at times. When I get scared or overwhelmed, God tells me to lean on Him. At first I didn't understand how to do this, but then my friend told me I don't really need to *do* anything. I just need to sit down and let God drive. If I rest and abide in Him, He can carry me and be the one in control. As the saying goes, "We may not know where we are going, but we know who is taking us there."

However, the truth is that I often let my fears get in the way of what God is doing. For example, fear of failure or fear of not being in control can cause me to distrust others. Just as Peter had to take that first step out of the boat, trusting the One who called him, so do we need to trust that God will protect and provide for our needs. His love for us is holy and good.

Are we willing to step out in obedience, trusting the One who calls us to follow Him, even though we can't always see where He is taking us? Or does fear threaten to take away the treasure God has chosen for us?

An illustration of this occurs in one of the final scenes of the movie *Indiana Jones and the Last Crusade*. Indiana Jones, played by Harrison Ford, is approaching a deep chasm which must be crossed in order to reach a great treasure. Even though he can only see an endless, dark abyss in front of him, he takes that bold step, trusting there is a pathway of some kind across that chasm, even though he can't see it. As I watched this scene in the movie, I felt myself gasp. Suddenly, his foot landed on a rocky bridge that appeared before him. The path had been there all along, but he couldn't see it until he made his first step.

Indiana Jones' first step forward must have taken all the faith he had. We also need to be bold and step forward in faith, knowing that we are standing on solid rock—the solid rock of Christ. He is the One we can totally depend upon! As it says in Isaiah 28:16, *"Behold, I lay in Zion a stone for a foundation, a tried stone, a precious cornerstone, a sure foundation"* (NKJV).

As M.L. Haskins wrote:

> I said to the man who stood at the gate of the year, "Give me a light that I may tread safely into the unknown." And he replied, "Go out into the darkness and put your hand into the hand of God.

That shall be to you better than light and safer
than a known way.[11]

Jesus says in John 10:10, "I have come that they may have
life, and that they may have it more abundantly" (NKJV).
However, many people, both Christians and non-Christians,
are hampered by fears that sneak into their daily lives and rob
them of this abundant life.

What is fear? It is an unpleasant emotion caused by the
belief that someone or something is dangerous or likely to
cause pain. It can also be the anxiety felt due to an unwel-
come event. There are both healthy fears and irrational fears.
An example of a healthy fear is one that occurs while in the
close proximity of a grizzly bear in the wild. Our healthy
fears can help to protect us.

However, fear can also prevent us from living the life that
God wants us to experience. For example, during my adult
years I developed an obsessive compulsive fear of germs.
Over time, I allowed this irrational fear to take root in my life
and it began to monopolize much of my thoughts, prevent-
ing me from living life to the fullest; it was like a shackle
around my ankles, hampering my daily walk. As it says in
Hebrews 12:1,

Therefore, since we are surrounded by such a
great cloud of witnesses, let us throw off everything that hinders and the sin that so easily entan-

---

[11] Haskins, Minnie Louise. *The Gate of the Year* (London, U.K.: Hodder
and Stoughton, 1940).

gles, and let us run with perseverance the race marked out for us. (NIV)

I discovered that my fear of germs was an outward sign that I didn't trust God with all my heart to direct my path straight or keep me safe. My fear signaled a deeply rooted inner problem. I wanted to be in control of my life because I was afraid of what might happen if I wasn't the one directing. However, God continued to encourage me to surrender my life more and more into His hands, and into His control. If He is Lord of my life, I need to let Him be *the* Lord of my life.

It has been said that the phrase "Do not fear" can be found in the Bible 365 times. This seems to speak loudly of the fact that fear is truly a daily struggle, especially considering that there are 365 days in the year. I also think this proves that God is very aware of all our fears, and wants us to walk free of this encumbrance.

Fear is also a sign that there are discrepancies in our faith. Dan tells a story from when he was in his twenties and was very distressed over the break-up of a relationship. After lamenting out loud once again, a friend of his bluntly responded, "You don't trust the God you say you serve!" Dan needed to fix his eyes on Jesus and trust that He would help him through his time of suffering.

> Therefore, since we are surrounded by such a great cloud of witnesses, let us throw off everything that hinders and the sin that so easily entangles, and let us run with perseverance the race marked out for us. Let us fix our eyes on Jesus,

the author and perfecter of our faith, who for the joy set before him endured the cross, scorning its shame, and sat down at the right hand of the throne of God. Consider him who endured such opposition from sinful men, so that you will not grow weary and lose heart. (Hebrews 12:1–3, NIV)

When we encounter fear, we can turn to God rather than letting it immobilize us and prevent us from moving in the direction He would have us go. Our weakness can be an opportunity to trust the Lord more rather than depending on our own strength. If we lean on God, and even let Him carry us, we will learn through our trials and grow in our faith. For it is through those struggles that we can learn and grow the most!

And He said to me, "My grace is sufficient for you, for My strength is made perfect in weakness." Therefore most gladly I will rather boast in my infirmities, that the power of Christ may rest upon me. Therefore I take pleasure in infirmities, in reproaches, in needs, in persecutions, in distresses, for Christ's sake. For when I am weak, then I am strong. (2 Corinthians 12:9–10, NKJV)

God will reward your faith. In the Bible,

the apostles said to the Lord, "Increase our faith."

So the Lord said, "If you have faith as a mustard seed, you can say to this mulberry tree, 'Be pulled up by the roots and be planted in the sea,' and it would obey you." (Luke 17:5–6, NKJV)

If God is telling you to do something, don't let fear stop you. You may experience fear while you step forward; that is part of our normal human experience. But step forward nonetheless. He will be faithful and reward you many times over. Remember, God has a purpose and He will not let you or anything else thwart His plan. He has a purpose and He will accomplish it with or without our cooperation. As it says in Isaiah 46:11,

Calling a bird of prey from the east,
the man of my counsel from a far country.
I have spoken, and I will bring it to pass;
I have purposed, and I will do it. (ESV)

Dan tells a true story of a pastor from Africa who was asked by God to write a book. The pastor said that God had given him a story that he needed to write and publish. It was his first book and he was surprised at how successful it was. He began to think he was a good writer and maybe he should write a second book. Then one day when he was praying, God told him, "You were my third choice. The first two chose not to write the book."

It was then that the pastor realized it was not his ability that had created the success, but rather God's message. He was simply God's messenger, and "third string" at that. He also realized that when God tells you to do something and you refuse, either because of fear or procrastination, you are causing God to choose someone else.

We need to step forward, despite our fears, and trust that God has a greater purpose, and that He will enable us to complete all that He has asked us to do. Moses and his brother Aaron are another example of this:

> Now it happened in the process of time that the king of Egypt died. Then the children of Israel groaned because of the bondage, and they cried out; and their cry came up to God because of the bondage. So God heard their groaning, and God remembered His covenant with Abraham, with Isaac, and with Jacob. And God looked upon the children of Israel, and God acknowledged them.
>
> Now Moses was tending the flock of Jethro his father-in-law, the priest of Midian. And he led the flock to the back of the desert, and came to Horeb, the mountain of God. And the Angel of the Lord appeared to him in a flame of fire from the midst of a bush. (Exodus 2:23–3:2, NKJV)

> And the Lord said: "I have surely seen the oppression of My people who are in Egypt, and have heard their cry because of their taskmasters, for I know their sorrows. So I have come down to deliver them out of the hand of the Egyptians, and to bring them up from that land to a good and

large land, to a land flowing with milk and honey…" (Exodus 3:7–8, NKJV)

God told Moses He had chosen him to go to Pharaoh and bring His people out of Egypt. He had chosen Moses to accomplish His purpose. However, six times Moses argued with God, questioning whether he was really the one to speak to the people of Israel. And in the end, God chose another man, Aaron, Moses' brother, to help him and speak for Him. This was not God's best, or first, plan. But God would not to be thwarted and did rescue His people out of Egypt, despite Moses' fears and initial disobedience.

How do we demonstrate our faith in God? We do this by obeying Him. Faith is an action word. God wants us to surrender more and more of our lives into His hands. This is not blind faith, but a choice to give up control and follow Him. It is a choice to surrender our lives into the hands of the One who knows us better than anyone else and has our best in mind.

One day, I spent two hours worrying about something that God had told me I had handled well. And yet I continued to worry and ignore what He had said to me. Whose voice was I listening to? Was it God's? Remember the Trust Game and how we need to distinguish between those different voices? Sometimes our self-talk is not accurate or healthy. Just think of all that lost energy! I had taken my focus off God and put it onto something unimportant and totally out of His will. This is like my fear of germs. It takes my focus off of Him and onto Satan, the "distractor."

Let us look again at Hebrews 12:1—

> Therefore, since we are surrounded by such a
> great cloud of witnesses, let us throw off every-
> thing that hinders and the sin that so easily entan-
> gles, and let us run with perseverance the race
> marked out for us. (NIV)

Clearly, this verse is saying that God wants us to be free of the sin that entangles our feet, because it slows us down and can cause us to trip and fall.

Life isn't easy. It is like a hard race. We would never enter a race wearing a heavy backpack! Fear is like a burdensome weight that slows down our progress in the race of life. We need to throw off that extra weight so that we can more easily run the race God has set out for us.

Then we are told, in Hebrews 12:2, to *"fix our eyes on Jesus"* (NIV). Rather than focusing on our sin or our troubles, we need to keep looking to our Lord. Talk to Him. Listen to Him. Focus on Jesus!

We will all encounter fear. Therefore, we need to know what to do when faced by it. My dog, Jake, is very frightened by thunderstorms. He is always tempted at those times to run away or chew something that doesn't belong to him. When I, his master, am with him during a storm, Jake is still somewhat afraid, but if he lies down near me, he does much better!

Just like Jake, we need to stay close to the Master at all times, especially during storms. When we are afraid, we shouldn't run from the Lord; we should draw near to Him. God doesn't promise to take away the storms. But we know that eventually the storm will subside. Like that Scott Krippayne song I quoted earlier, "Sometimes He calms the storm, and other times He calms His child."

Step out in faith. Trust that God will give you what you need to accomplish His purposes. He is faithful and will not ask us to do something unless He intends to provide the strength and resources we need at that moment to accomplish His purposes.

Doesn't the Bible tell us that *"Abraham believed God, and it was accounted to him for righteousness"* (Romans 4:3, NKJV)? It was not Abraham's works that resulted in his righteousness. Rather, his faith was belief lived out in obedience, and this was credited to Him as righteousness:

> By faith Abraham obeyed when he was called to go out to the place which he would receive as an inheritance. And he went out not knowing where he was going. By faith he dwelt in the land of promise as in a foreign country, dwelling in tents with Isaac and Jacob, the heirs with him of the same promise; for he waited for the city which has foundations, whose builder and maker is God.
>
> By faith Sarah herself also received strength to conceive seed, and she bore a child when she was past the age, because she judged Him faithful who had promised. Therefore from one man, and him as good as dead, were born as many as the stars of the sky in multitude—innumerable as the sand which is by the seashore. (Hebrews 11:8–12, NKJV)

He will bring along the men, the strength, the wisdom, and the keys to accomplishing His purpose. "He preserves the souls of His saints; He delivers them out of the hand of the wicked" (Psalm 97:10, NKJV).

Calling a bird of prey from the east,
the man of my counsel from a far country.
I have spoken, and I will bring it to pass;
I have purposed, and I will do it.
(Isaiah 46:11, ESV)

God did all these things as He created the earth, and yet, as Bible teacher J. Vernon McGee says:

How many people today are attempting to run their lives as if they were God? They feel that they don't need God, and they live without Him. The interesting thing is that when God made us He did not put a steering wheel on any of us. Why? Because He wants to guide our lives. He wants us to come to Him for salvation first, and then He wants to take charge of our lives. When you and I run our lives, we are in the place of God. We are in the driver's seat. We are the ones who are the captains of our own little ships or our own little planes, and we are going through the water or the air just to suit ourselves. That is pride, and anyone who reaches that position, if he continues in it, is committing a sin which is fatal because it means he will go into a lost eternity.[12]

Be content with having less control. We can do this by trusting God and by respecting His wisdom to lead well. He is the Almighty, with all power and wisdom. He is worthy of our praise and respect. He is not always doing what we might expect, for He often works through the unexpected, but if we walk very close to the Lord we won't get lost, just like the example of the dog and his master.

Let me draw an analogy to explain this concept further. One day, as I was driving on a busy highway through our city, a large flatbed semi pulled into the lane beside me. I realized I was nervous to drive beside this large vehicle; my inclination was to stay as far over to the left as possible.

Now, I want you to compare this experience to our spiritual walk. God doesn't want us to pull away from Him in fear, but encourages us to stay close to Him, where we will be protected and can more closely follow His ways.

As my exit neared, I was tempted to pull ahead of this truck. But we shouldn't get in the way of what God is doing. It is best to follow His lead and not get in front of Him. Keep your eyes on Him. We will get into less trouble if we stay close to the Master.

There is certainly less control from our position in the rear. We may have a hard time seeing around God to see where we are going, and when He slows down we are forced

---

[12] McGee, J. Vernon. *Edited Messages on Obadiah*. As quoted in "May I Say" Monthly Ministry Report of Thru the Bible Radio Network, May 2010 (Pasadena, CA: Thru the Bible Radio Network, 2010), pp. 1–2.

to slow down, too. This is the best spot to be in—protected from the rush of the world, following the God who knows well how to lead.

Our friend, Tim George, a teacher at our local church, once stated, "Nothing is as refreshing as knowing someone else is in control—and then sitting back and enjoying the ride."

God is all-knowing, and knows exactly what I need. I knew that I needed to release control of my entire life into His hands. In order to do this, I first needed to realize that God loves me unconditionally. I knew that Dan and Justin had always loved me in this way. Could I go one step further and accept that God loved me even more unconditionally than my husband and son ever had?

We know how much we love our children or our spouse. But do we realize that God loves us so much more than we could ever imagine and wants to guide us every step of the way? Knowing that God is our ever-loving Father, we can trust Him to care for us and keep us from harm, just as a parent loves and protects their child. But even more so! For as it says in Isaiah 64:4, *"Since before time began no one has ever imagined, no ear heard, no eye seen, a God like you who works for those who wait for him"* (The Message).

We discussed in the previous chapter the belief that God really does love you. He has reached out and touched your life so many times with the tiny butterflies in your life. God's love came first, for He has always loved us.

Know that the Lord is God.
It is he who made us, and we are his;

we are his people, the sheep of his pasture.
Enter his gates with thanksgiving
and his courts with praise;
give thanks to him and praise his name.
For the Lord is good and his love endures
forever;
his faithfulness continues through all
generations.
(Psalm 100:3–5, NIV)

If you are questioning whether God really loves you, consider this: if you were thinking about dating or even marrying someone, you would want to be sure they were the right one. You would want to be certain that you loved them and they loved you! By spending time with that person, you would soon discover the truth. The same holds true for God. Spend time with God and you will discover the truth of His love for you.

If you are afraid to learn that God truly loves you, you may find yourself avoiding time with Him. I challenge you to be bold and courageous, and to discover the truth!

You can spend time with God by going for walks or drives together—just you and God. You might choose to bring your pet along, as long as he doesn't distract you from focusing on God. You can spend time with Him by finding a favorite spot that is just for the two of you.

Whether it is summer or winter, fall or spring, we need to feed our longing souls with the food of God. Only He can feed our heart, soul, and mind so that it is truly satisfied. Find a quiet spot where you can spend time in the Bible, time in prayer, and time in silence. It is when we are silent that we can hear God's words for us, personally. This is how you will reach out for God. Remember those butterflies—He is already reaching out for you.

Jesus is always our best example. Time and time again, Jesus went off alone to pray and spend time with the Father. As we learn to accept the love of God, our fears begin to evaporate. We begin to trust Him as we learn more about His true character.

When Justin's twentieth birthday approached, two and a half years after he passed away, God said to me, "Forgive Me." There was a moment's hesitation, as I thought about how I really wished He hadn't taken my son to heaven. I chose to forgive Him, partly because I knew the bitterness would destroy me, and partly because I knew God loved me and I could trust Him. Through spending quality time with Him each day, I had grown to love and really trust God. For the first time, I felt I could truly forgive and was able to honestly admit that His reasons for taking my son must have been good ones. That might sound a bit surprising to some, but if you have experienced a tremendous loss in your life, you will likely understand the emotions that can lead us to blame God for our pain. I love my son so much that it is incredibly hard at times to be apart from him. But I know that God must have His reasons, and because I know He loves me I choose to trust what He is doing. *"For God has not given us the spirit of fear, but of power and of love and of a sound mind"* (2 Timothy 1:7, NKJV).

Choosing to lay down control and forgive God was a huge step—one that I didn't even realize I needed to take until that moment! I had to take my fear of losing control and put it into His hands. God would know what to do next, even if I didn't. The most important thing I needed to do was trust Him. Then I could go forward. Then I could let Him lead.

"Where are we going now, God?" I asked.

"Somewhere exciting, my daughter!" said the Lord. "Somewhere exciting!"

In summary, we need to trust God and obey. God has a plan and purpose for His children, and He may choose you to bring this about. We need to be willing to let God drive, and to step forward in faith, knowing He will direct and enable us to do the job. Arguing with God will not thwart His plan; it will only cause Him to choose someone else.

Wouldn't you love to be the one to serve God in a new and exciting way? Step forward, even though you may not be able to see what is ahead. Don't worry, you're not the one driving. God is!

If we choose to continue in life doing nothing about the fear we are carrying each and every day, we risk losing our health, for it is well-documented that habitual fear causes illness and disease. Fear can eat away your insides. But God offers us freedom from fear.

As we fully accept that God truly loves us, we can learn to trust Him more deeply, and in turn discover that we want to let Him lead. As we grow in faith, our love for Him grows, too.

Step out in faith and trust that He will take care of the details! God is in control—put your life fully into His hands. Letting God drive is absolutely amazing! Who knows where

He might take you? "It's all part of the adventure!" my husband says. Wow! What an adventure!

CHAPTER ELEVEN
God Embraces Our Suffering

Listen to me, you stubborn of heart,
you who are far from righteousness:
I bring near my righteousness; it is not far off,
and my salvation will not delay;
I will put salvation in Zion,
for Israel my glory.

—ISAIAH 46:12–13 (ESV)

The sorrows of Sheol surrounded me;
The snares of death confronted me.
In my distress I called upon the Lord,
And cried out to my God;
He heard my voice from His temple,
And my cry came before Him, even to His ears."

—PSALM 18:5–6 (NKJV)

11

All of us will grieve someday, for:

Many have died.
Many have grieved.
Many have loved.
Many have lost loved ones.

New life will reappear.
Spring comes after the winter.

These words were spoken to me by the Holy Spirit as I walked with our dog through an open field, only a few months after the death of our son.

Grieving is a long process and, for most, a difficult cross to bear. And yet death and loss are an experience common to all. All of us will eventually lose a loved one due to death. Others will experience loss through divorce, and still others will have to say goodbye to the way things used to be, due to an illness or trauma in their life or the life of a loved one.

Consolation vs. Desolation

Sometimes our mind resists entering into deep sorrow, for grief takes a great deal of physical and emotional energy. We need courage to enter into such a dark crucible. There are times when I have the need to cry and my tears flow easily. At other times my body tenses, as though I am resisting entering into deep sorrow. Consider, too, that our culture discourages weakness and displays of sadness, and often encourages people experiencing grief to stay busy. All these factors work together, causing many to avoid deep grief.

But God's ways are not like our own. He calls us to move inward, closer to Him, and to move forward. I have found that He wants us to face the real depth and reason for our grief, which means entering into the grief rather than trying to avoid it. Jesus suffered while here on earth; He understands our human condition. By entering into suffering, we move towards Christ and identify with His pain and suffering.

Acceptance is a process; these changes do not come overnight. Some days I am more successful in acknowledging my weaknesses than others. Although I still long for my dear son, God is gentle in how He draws me forward.

St. Ignatius speaks of the concepts of "consolation" and "desolation." He explains that in consolation we move closer to God, whereas in desolation we move away from Him.

I was first introduced to this concept in June 2008, only four months after our son passed away. My spiritual director,[13] after explaining the difference between these two states, helped me to experience, through silence, a new taste of consolation. Her advice to me was to move close to God in my times of grief and sorrow by saying, "Father, I know You are here in this with me." By saying these words, I found my grief came to the surface and, more importantly, I was able to sense God's nearness in my pain. Sometimes this also enabled me to cry more freely.

As Stephen Verney states in his book, *Into the New Age*:

> This is the nature of the encounter, not that I am stumbling towards the Abba Father, but that the Abba Father is running towards me. It is not that I love God but that God believes in me. The discovery at the heart of contemplation is not that I am contemplating the divine love, but that the divine love is contemplating me. He sees me and understands and accepts me, He has compassion on me, He creates me afresh from moment to moment, and He protects me and is with me through death and into life beyond.[14]

---

[13] A "spiritual director" is a Christian individual who has taken a formal course of study in Spiritual Direction. Christian Spiritual Direction is a relationship where one person is helped by another through prayerful listening to discern more fully God's presence and direction in their life. See *The Practice of Spiritual Direction*, by Wm. Barry and Wm. Connolly.

[14] Verney, Stephen. Into the New Age (Nashville, TN: Zondervan, 1976), pp. 91–92.

How like the story of the Prodigal Son this is, in which the father was grieving and missing his son and kept watch for his return. When finally his son returned to him broken, the father ran to greet him, kissed him, and blessed him with gifts and a feast in his honor.

In John 11:35, we read that Jesus wept when His dear friend Lazarus died. How amazing that our Lord, who knew He would soon raise this very man from the dead, was allowing Himself to weep in front of others. His grief was not hidden. Jesus did not wear a tough mask to hide himself from those who gathered there that day.

We, too, must walk truthfully along the path of our struggles. I try to let my tears flow while in the midst of a culture that has a tough exterior. I am learning this lesson with God's help.

Surely God will bless us, as He promises to bring good out of all circumstances (Romans 8:28). Yet in our lives we will encounter many trials and much suffering. We will have the opportunity to see Christ throughout all circumstances— to see Him in others, to see Him in His creation, and to see Him through pain and love.

I have found that:

> Grieving is a time of sadness
> When there is a hole in our heart.
> And yet Christ must be the whole of
> our heart.

> Tearfully, we take His hand so as not to
> stumble.
> Joyfully, we adore Him and accept His help.

God's Comfort

About four months after Justin's passing, when his eighteenth birthday was about three weeks away, sadness and anger began to grip my heart. I felt angry with God and even took it out on our dog one day. How foolish of me! Deep down, I wanted some sense of control in a situation where I had none!

Finally, I stopped fighting and went to sleep. In the morning, God's mercy was there for me; I had peace to start off my day. As it says in Lamentations 3:23, His mercies are new every morning.

When I went for a walk with my dog that morning through the woods near our home, I listened to God and He directed me to take the path on the right. This was not my usual route, but thankfully I obeyed His promptings.

I began to feel another wave of sadness and grief. Rather than reacting with my gut response of, "Oh no! Here comes the grief—brace yourself," I tried to be more sensitive to God and to what He was doing in that moment. My eyes fell to the ground, and there was a single green leaf in the middle of the path; it was heart-shaped! God's love came to my mind at that moment. I listened to Him further. God told me that He understood, and that He loves me and knew I love Him. I felt His peace return; He had taken me from intense sorrow back into His peace.

God's comfort is always sufficient. But we must be prepared and willing to walk through the grief He has placed in our lives. Justin's death forced me to learn this difficult lesson. I love him dearly and miss him so much that, at times, it hurts terribly. But by turning to God in prayer, often through silence and listening, or through His Word, I have found daily comfort.

Later that day, I opened my Bible and found myself looking at Psalm 5:1–3:

> Give ear to my words, O Lord,
> Consider my meditation.
> Give heed to the voice of my cry,
> My King and my God,
> For to You I will pray.
> My voice You shall hear in the morning, O Lord;
> In the morning I will direct it to You,
> And I will look up. (NKJV)

And so I tried looking up to God. Where else can our help come from? (Psalm 121:2) Our *"God is our refuge and strength, an ever-present help in trouble"* (Psalm 46:1, NIV).

Carrying

Ten months after my son passed away, God taught me another lesson in this long process of grieving. At that time, I would periodically think of Justin with a sense of regret that we were no longer together. God's response to this was twofold. First, He wanted me to stop and listen carefully to Him. Secondly, He told me that He wanted to carry me.

At that point, God gave me a picture in my mind of a long-forgotten childhood storybook character, Thumbelina, who was sitting on a leaf. Thumbelina is a Hans Christian Andersen character who was given this name because she was the size of a thimble. I instantly made the connection to myself who, tiny in comparison to God, could easily be carried by Him. I realized that all I needed to do when God said He wanted to carry me was picture little Thumbelina sitting safely upon a leaf and remember that God is more than able to carry me.

But first, I must sit down and trust that God will take care of the details. This concept of sitting down was not altogether new to me, for in Watchman Nee's book *Sit, Walk, Stand*, he states,

> For Christianity begins not with a big DO, but with a big DONE. Thus Ephesians opens with the statement that God has "blessed us with every spiritual blessing in the heavenly places in Christ" and we are invited at the very outset to sit down and enjoy what God has done for us; not to set out to try and attain it for ourselves...
>
> Until a man does this he is no Christian; for to say: "I can do nothing to save myself; but by His grace God has done everything for me in Christ", is to take the first step in the life of faith. The Christian life from start to finish is based upon this principle of utter dependence upon the Lord

Jesus. There is no limit to the grace God is willing to bestow upon us. He will give us everything, but we can receive none of it except as we rest in Him. "Sitting" is an attitude of rest. Something has been finished, work stops, and we sit. It is paradoxical, but true, that we only advance in the Christian life as we learn first of all to sit down.

What does it really mean to sit down? When we walk or stand we bear on our legs all the weight of our own body, but when we sit down our entire weight rests upon the chair or couch on which we sit. We grow weary when we walk or stand, but we feel rested when we have sat down for a while. In walking or standing we ex-pend a great deal of energy, but when we are seated we relax at once, because the strain no longer falls upon our muscles and nerves but upon something outside of ourselves. So also in the spiritual realm, to sit down is simply to rest our whole weight—our load, ourselves, our fu-ture, everything—upon the Lord. We let Him bear the responsibility and cease to carry it our-selves.[15]

For Paul tells us in Ephesians 2:4–6,

But God is so rich in mercy, and he loved us so much, that even though we were dead because of

---

[15] Nee, Watchman. *Sit, Walk, Stand* (Wheaton, IL: Tyndale House Publishers, Inc., 1962), pp. 14–15.

our sins, he gave us life when he raised Christ from the dead. (It is only by God's grace that you have been saved!) For he raised us from the dead along with Christ and seated us with him in the heavenly realms because we are united with Christ Jesus. (NLT)

We are seated with Christ in the heavenly places here and now, not when we die. Christ's work on the cross is done, and I don't have to DO anything to earn His love or His help. He loves me now and wants to help me today. When I feel overwhelmed by my grief or unable to move forward, I can ask the Lord to help me. Sometimes His response is to offer to carry me. My job then is to merely rest in Him and to be open to the gift He is offering me.

I must confess that sometimes I want to resist God's offer of rest or peace, because I am still angry or want to stay sad, or perhaps I don't know how to bring myself to accept His help. But God understands. He created our emotions; He knows exactly how to help us. He only asks us to sit, just as Watchman Nee explained. God has already done the work through Christ on the cross, and now He is asking us to sit down in the palm of His hand.

One day I was really struggling against God's offer to carry me. I was upset and missing Justin and felt overwhelmed by the enormity of my loss. As a loving Father, God was patiently offering me rest and comfort and love. It was as if He was right there in front of me, holding His arms open. Would I choose to take that step forward and accept what God was offering?

Tentatively, I said aloud, "Okay, Lord, You will have to do this! I can't do it!" and I imagined myself in His big arms. Consciously, I tried not to struggle, but to rest there. Immediately, the tears came and I allowed them to flow. Just as the Prodigal Son eventually realized he needed his father, so did I finally realize that I needed to run toward my heavenly Father.

Then the words "Throughout the journey" came to me. Yes, I needed to let Him carry me throughout the journey.

> I would have lost heart, unless I had believed
> That I would see the goodness of the Lord
> In the land of the living.
> Wait on the Lord;
> Be of good courage,
> And He shall strengthen your heart;
> Wait, I say, on the Lord!
> (Psalm 27:13–14, NKJV)

God allows difficulties to come into our lives. He has not promised a journey free of struggle or pain, but rather He is offering to carry us through this difficult journey. As Kathy Legg, my sister-in-law and one of my editors, says, "God allows, God comforts, and God restores." I believe this is true; our God allows trials and struggles to come into our lives. He comforts us through those difficult times. He restores us, lifting us out of the dark valley and placing us upon a bright hill where we can see our way forward once again.

The Daily Walk

God wants us to learn to rely on Him, to trust Him for our daily bread. But in order to do so, we must first put all our faith in Him.

Faith demands action. In order to truly have faith in something, we must put our faith into action by stepping forward into what we know to be true. We put shoe leather to our beliefs and do what we say we believe. In fact, the word "believe" means to depend, to rely, to trust. It is a word of action.

"To look for God's handiwork only in the spectacular means you miss out on His provision for you each and every day," says Sheila Barlow in *Stepping through My Nightmares*.[16] We need to learn to walk with Him in the everyday.

Bonnie Thomas, daughter-in-law of Capernwray's founder, reminds us that sometimes we want God to give us the mountaintop experience rather than the daily walk. We must learn to lean on the Lord each day and rely on Him for our daily bread; just like manna, He will give us a daily portion that is sufficient.

Speaking at a ladies' retreat, she explained, "Jesus is the Good Shepherd who lays down His life for the sheep. He is worthy of our trust. He leads us like sheep; He doesn't drive us like cattle. Our worth, as sheep, is demonstrated by the price that was paid for us—His life. Jesus is our home until He takes us home."

---

[16] Barlow, Sheila. *Stepping through My Nightmares* (UK: Eagle Publishing, 2002), p. 198.

This means learning to spend time with Him throughout the day. God is always home and listening. You just need to be open to Him. One way to do this is to pray throughout the day, to have a running conversation with God all the time. However, a conversation is two-way. Remember to be open to what God is saying, and give Him equal "air time."

I find it is very easy to let the concerns and busyness of my life push aside those valuable chunks of time I could spend reading the Bible. A dear friend used to tell me about a mother whose children had learned to show respect when their mother shut herself into the bathroom—they knew she was spending time alone with The King!

Our daily walk with God is very much affected by how we spend our time. When we are in mourning, we need to allow time to grieve and time to rest. How thankful I was for my husband, who still understands this and has never pushed me to go back to work as a schoolteacher. My work has always been in the home: mentoring women, leading Bible studies, teaching a Suzuki Early Childhood music class, and now writing.

I soon discovered how blessed I was to be at home, taking the time to grieve fully. However, this is not our culture's way. Many who work outside the home are not given ample time off work to grieve fully, and many feel they have to rush back to work in order to keep busy. I can't count how many times I was asked the question "Are you keeping busy?" during the months immediately following our son's death.

There were times when I knew I wasn't even fit to go back to work. As my husband wisely said one day, "Diane, if you were working right now, you'd be fired!" He was right!

The first year and a half after Justin's death, I found I couldn't focus or remember facts clearly, and I was often tired due to my grief. I admire those who have the strength and energy to carry both their grief and their workplace duties, and even care for children or other family members.

What did I do with my time? I can say now, looking back, that it was tempting to "be busy," even in my own home. But the best things I did with my time were to:

a) sleep lots, including naps during the day. (Grieving is exhausting!)
b) go for daily walks with my dog and talk with God along the way. (We often had our best conversations on those walks!)
c) write in my journal about everything on my mind, and about what God is saying to me.
d) pray with friends and mentors.
e) listen to God in silence throughout the day, and when I awoke in the middle of the night.

Of course, there were many things to do around the house as well. But these were five things that had the most positive and lasting effect on my journey.

Mourning through the Arts

All of us will grieve, but only some of us will mourn. Grief is the sadness and loss we all feel upon losing a loved one. But only some will seek ways to express their grief through mourning. For example, some mourn through tears, others through journaling, and still others through the arts.

I put together a memory album of photos, words, and sympathy cards shortly after our son died. One of our respite workers helped me with this album, which was a wonderful way to heal and remember Justin. I also created a quilt-like painting composed of small four-inch squares, each depicting a different event that had occurred in the weeks and months around the time of Justin's passing. For example, one tiny painting held the words "Justin might not make it" and another showed a butterfly and the phrases, "Like a butterfly, no longer confined to your wheelchair" and "Flying free of your hospital cocoon..." These small paintings were then pasted onto a large blue background in a checkerboard pattern, resembling a quilt. This project was a wonderfully expressive way of mourning that enabled me to honor the many ways God had touched our lives during that time.

Another way I expressed mourning was through dance. Only six months after our son passed away, God brought me to a liturgical dance workshop for the first time in my life. Although I was shy to take part initially, I soon found there was no pressure or judgment from others to dance in a particular way. I was free to move and dance, often with my eyes closed to block out the others in the room. I discovered a new and beautiful way to communicate and worship God. In time, He turned my mourning into dancing (Psalm 30:11).

Dance was a part of worshipping God during Old Testament times. In the Book of Exodus, *"Moses and the children of Israel sang [a] song to the Lord"* (Exodus 15:1, NKJV) after God saved them from the Egyptians by parting the Red Sea. Right after this song, *"Miriam the prophetess, the sister of Aaron [and Moses], took the timbrel in her hand; and all the women went out after her with timbrels and with dances"* (Exodus 15:20, NKJV). What a joyous celebration!

Dance became a part of my second Mother's Day without Justin. There at the graveside, God prompted me to dance with my veil to one of my favorite songs, "Mighty to Save," by Laura Story, in which she sings about how God has conquered the grave. Up until that day, I had often danced to this song in my home and pictured the cold, hard gravel that had covered my son's grave during that first winter and early spring after we buried him. On that warm Mother's Day, God brought healing to my heart as I danced to this song. God was visibly there with me that day as He picked up my veil in the breeze and moved it in waves across the green grass. The joyous colors of my pink and yellow veil flowed above the green grass of summer, and the cold, painful picture of gravel over my son's grave was replaced with a new one. That day, I experienced Justin's new life and God's love for me.

Our God is a living God who interacts with us today; He is alive, not dead. My son, too, is alive and well in heaven today.

> This is what God the LORD says—he who created the heavens and stretched them out, who spread out the earth and all that comes out of it, who gives breath to its people, and life to those who walk on it: "I, the Lord, have called you in

righteousness; I will take hold of your hand."
(Isaiah 42:5–6a, NIV)

Confronting the Grief Head-On

Many of us will dread the arrival of anniversaries, birthdays,
and holidays after the loss of a loved one. These times can be
especially poignant. Some will also grieve the coming of different seasons, especially as this triggers special memories. I
discovered this during the first summer after our son died
when we boldly went to the lake where we had always spent
a week of holiday time together as a family.

For many days, Dan and I avoided one of our favorite activities to do with our son. As our week drew to a close, I
knew we needed to face the grief head-on. So I asked Dan to
help me take the inner tube out into the water, just as we had
done with Justin many times before. Finally, my tears came.
Rather than holding them in, I chose to let them flow. I then
felt at peace again.

When autumn arrived, I found myself grieving again, as
school buses came and went along our street that year without Justin. Again God blessed me during this time by challenging me to boldly go to his school one day. Not knowing
what to expect, I found myself tense and nervous as I anticipated my visit. However, upon arrival, I found I was fine, and
God showed me that He was carrying me.

I had decided it would be just fine if I cried that day.
Really, it would be quite natural if I did. However, as it
turned out, I didn't need to. As I faced a child's empty wheelchair, I pushed it a little and then sat down in it myself. Later,

I even got to participate in the Terry Fox Run by pushing one of Justin's classmates outside in his wheelchair with great joy and speed!

God had blessings in that day for me, blessings I could never have anticipated. I would never have experienced those blessings if I had not confronted my fears and gone to the school that day. As the season of fall continued, I saw more beauty in the colors around me and I heard more than one person mention how God doesn't just let fall come in browns, but in reds and yellows and oranges! It seemed He was letting the words of others draw me into the gifts He had prepared for me.

As autumn extended long through the entire month of October with warm days, warm enough for me to work in my flower garden, I reveled in His blessings and discovered fall to be not just a season of dying but a season of color and richness.

When we first marry, we are in the spring season of our marriage. As we raise our children, we move into summer. As our children leave home, we find ourselves in the autumn of our relationship as husband and wife. Finally, when we enter our senior years, we come into the winter of our lives.

As a mother of a handicapped child, I had always assumed we would just stay in the summer season of our life, for I thought we would always be caring for Justin. Then one day I realized we had entered autumn, for our son had gone on ahead of us.

> He has sent Me to heal the brokenhearted,
> To proclaim liberty to the captives...

To comfort all who mourn,
To console those who mourn in Zion,
To give them beauty for ashes,
The oil of joy for mourning,
The garment of praise for the spirit of heaviness;
That they may be called trees of righteousness,
The planting of the Lord,
That He may be glorified.
(Isaiah 61:1–3, NKJV)

Another occasion in which I confronted my grief head-on occurred about a month after Justin passed away. As I drove across the city, I felt God bringing to my mind the Children's Hospital and the name of one of his doctors. I sensed He was asking me to go to the hospital where our son had died and thank this very special doctor who had cared for him during his final illness. Naturally, I was hesitant to do this and wanted to be sure that this was really what God was asking me to do. So I prayed a little prayer, asking that if this was God's will that He bring the Children's Hospital to my mind again when I was done my errands that day. He did. As soon as I started heading home, the hospital came to my mind again. I realized then that I needed to go boldly forward and do what He was prompting me to do, despite my nervousness and fears.

So I drove to the hospital and went in to visit the ward where Justin had spent about twenty-four hours before going down to the ICU. Although there were times when the tears flowed down my face, everyone was happy I had come. Those who had served our family during that short time recognized me and came over to offer their condolences. One of my favorite nurses, who had served us diligently on a previous stay in the hospital, was there, too. I was able to thank each one for all their wonderful care. I was able to write a little thank-you note for our nurse, Stephanie, who had been in charge of our son's care before he was transferred to the ICU. I wanted her to know how much we had appreciated her devotion and wonderful care for our son.

Then, as I looked towards the desk on the unit, I saw the doctor God had brought to my mind earlier that morning. I was able to speak to her and thank her for her extraordinary care and compassion. In response, she commented how unusual it was for me to have come at that particular time, as she only worked part-time and was filling in for another doctor that day. God knew that, and had directed my steps.

I went back to the Children's Hospital on other occasions after that. One time, I had a piece of equipment to return to the Seating Clinic where they help children with the seating systems of their wheelchairs. How thankful I was that the person they paged to come out and receive this equipment from me was the very woman who had overseen the repair and adjustment of Justin's wheelchair on many occasions. I took the opportunity to thank her for the way in which she and her co-workers had made me feel a part of their team.

One day, I went into the ICU itself. I didn't know what would happen while I was there, but again God had blessings planned for me. The secretary at the ICU reception desk recognized me and asked how I was. Then one of the doctors who had supervised our son's care came over to talk to me. She made a point of asking what I needed from them. I said I wasn't sure, but then agreed to go down to Justin's room. She walked me there herself and we talked along the way.

When I got to his room, there across the hall was one of our favorite ICU nurses. Rob seemed a little surprised to see me, but remained quiet while I entered the room. The doctor and I closed the curtains, giving me privacy, and then she left me alone. I was not sure what I would encounter there in terms of emotions, but what I did discover was that any fears I might have had earlier were unwarranted. I felt total peace and a sense of quiet in that room. So I left quietly and said goodbye at the desk.

A few weeks after Mother's Day in May 2009, my birthday arrived. It brought on a great deal of emotion for me, especially anger. I was a bit surprised by this, but the grieving cycle is like a circle around which we will travel more than once, encountering a variety of emotions in no particular order.

It was interesting to note that again I heard someone's sincere concern for me expressed in the question, "Are you keeping busy?" I knew this wasn't the answer, for it would only serve to prevent me from walking through this dark valley that God had placed in my life. I had come to accept that some would understand what I was going through and others would not. Everyone processes grief differently, and some haven't yet experienced what it is like to lose a loved one. Someday it will be my turn to listen and be compassionate.

God gave me the courage to confront my tears head-on and tell a dear friend that I just wanted to celebrate my birthday like we always had—with Dan and Justin and me having chocolate cake together. All through my life, I had celebrated birthdays with chocolate cake and family around me. Just to say this out loud to my friend brought me to tears. I needed to say it. Finally, at the end of the day, tired from busyness, I realized what I really needed to do was bake that chocolate cake. So courageously, I baked a favorite recipe I had used many times for birthdays. As I bit into a piece of warm cake, I began to feel this latest wave of grief subsiding. Not to say that food should be the solution to our grief! I am just saying that sometimes we need to be bold and go forward into what makes us cry the hardest, because we miss it so much! Rather than avoiding it, we should do it!

Why Bother?

Some may ask why bother with all of this? Why not just get on with life and leave the grief behind? *If* that were possible, it might be a great option, even though we'd miss out on what grief teaches. Grief won't just disappear at our bidding. It must either be lived consciously or buried unconsciously.

Those who bury their grief may find it comes back years later with a vengeance. It will be much harder to deal with at a later date. Buried grief is like a wound that has scabbed over, but the underlying infection has never fully cleared up. The ugly pus of the wound is still lying under the surface, just out of sight. We still carry it and God knows it is there.

I discovered this in my adult years when Justin was fifteen years old. He and I had been praying about getting a dog for some months, when suddenly one day I had the sense that "our" dog was at the SPCA. I told Dan this, and he went onto their website. They had many dogs available, but only two attracted Dan's eye. One was a lab-hound cross named Jake. When Dan, Justin, Keith (our respite worker), and I went to the SPCA we requested to meet Jake. We were directed into a penned area in which we could spend some time with him.

However, I was not prepared for what was to occur next. When they brought Jake into our pen, I couldn't stop staring at him, despite Dan's attempts to get my attention and help with the task at hand. I told Dan that I needed a minute to collect my thoughts outside.

Once outside, I realized I was very upset and in shock. This dog looked very much like my childhood Great Dane, Sheba, who had died suddenly when I was very young. Both dogs were black with some white on their chest. Both were slim, long-legged dogs with long tails. The difference was that Jake had floppy ears while Sheba had sharp, pointed ears.

Once I had collected my thoughts, I went back inside and we decided after some discussion to put this dog "on hold" for a day, so we could consider our decision further. That evening, we decided we would adopt Jake, and the next day Keith, Justin, and I went to pick him up. Justin was chattering away in the back seat while we drove to the SPCA. It was Keith who realized he was trying to say Jake's name. "Gake, Gake, Gake," he kept repeating. Justin was very excited about our new dog, and this was the first time he had spoken a new word in years!

What I didn't know was that Jake was to be the catalyst in a long process of grieving that had never occurred during my childhood. Our Great Dane had suddenly disappeared and died when I was a young girl. Sheba's quiet nature and our daily walks had been a treasure to me during childhood, for when my oldest sister went off to university I had taken over her care. As I looked back on Sheba's death, I remembered being at our lakeside cabin when she just disappeared one morning before we all woke up. We called and called and looked for her along the quiet, wooded paths near our cabin. Dad even took my brother and sister and me out in the boat to look for her. She was nowhere to be found. Dad said that she probably went back into the woods to die, as some animals will do this when they know they are dying.

We went on with our lives. I know I never really grieved the loss of Sheba or marked her death in any way. I was young and didn't realize the importance of this, and that was what our family chose to do.

Now, almost forty years later, I was faced with a very strong emotional reaction that just wouldn't go away. Suddenly, after adopting Jake, I had a very short temper, with the littlest things setting me off on a regular basis. I had little patience for our new dog and often took my anger out on him. There was a hurt there that needed to be healed, and I am positive that God chose Jake, a dog that looked like Sheba but was strong-willed rather than meek, to help me face my forgotten grief.

Years later, I feel healed from this scabbed-over pain and I love walking every day with Jake. He has become a devoted companion. I have also learned the importance of marking a death, of crying when someone you love dies, and of grieving for as long as you need. I have learned that grieving matters to God, whether it is due to the loss of a spouse resulting from divorce, or the death of a friend or relative—or even the loss of a beloved pet. I know God helped us to adopt not just any dog, but a dog that looked like Sheba and who would bring on the grief I had unknowingly buried forty years earlier. God wants us to be whole and fully healed.

The Waves of Grief

I want you to know that the grief will continue, often showing up when you least expect it. For some, it will be there for the rest of your lives. This is normal, not unhealthy, as some would have you believe.

Just the other day, my very strong eighty-one-year-old father suddenly experienced a strong wave of grief and tears, as something brought to mind his wife (my mother), who had passed away eleven years before. Dad said he hadn't experienced tears of grief like that in probably two or three years. He said he just had to let the tears come, and let them flow.

God doesn't promise to remove your suffering but wants you to embrace it, just as He does.

Remember, Jesus wept; you will weep, too. Jesus suffered, and so will you.

God allows suffering, for it is there in that deep crucible that you are forced to lean more upon Him.

"Then Jesus said to His disciples, 'If anyone desires to come after Me, let him deny himself, and take up his cross, and follow Me'" (Matthew 16:24, NKJV). Those who are experiencing suffering have a cross to bear. Don't walk around your pain, avoiding your cross. Bend down, asking God to help you pick it up. Jesus does not say He will take your cross away; rather, He tells you to pick up your cross of suffering and bring it with you, for your pain and sorrow will be a part of your journey.

Jesus also says,

> Come to Me, all you who labor and are heavy
> laden, and I will give you rest. Take My yoke
> upon you and learn from Me, for I am gentle and
> lowly in heart, and you will find rest for your
> souls. For my yoke is easy and My burden is light.
> (Matthew 11:28–30, NKJV)

Jesus wants us only to bear the load He gives us. Sometimes we worry and make our load heavier than it needs to be, taking on more than He wants us to carry. Other times we try to take the burden on by ourselves. But Jesus says, *"Take My yoke upon you."* He also says that His yoke will be easy and His burden light.

Picture a small ox and a big ox, each yoked to the same burden. They pull this load together, but the bigger ox bears the greater portion of the load. Jesus wants to carry the heaviest portion of your load.

If you surrender your pain and troubles into His hands, you will find that what seemed impossible is not. For He says that *"nothing is impossible with God"* (Luke 1:37, NIV).

Jesus also says, *"Take my yoke upon you and learn from Me."* There is much to learn along this road of suffering—maybe humility or compassion for others.

I have a relative who was in a car accident. His condition has deteriorated to the point where he now rarely communicates with others and is dependent upon others for his basic needs. Some might wonder, what is the point in him living anymore? But God may have a purpose for his life, for through his condition others can learn patience, empathy, and love.

God wants to direct us through our troubled times. Let Him drive. Jesus says there will be rest in the journey if you take the yoke He gives you.

We may not want to stay in the crucible of suffering long enough for God to speak to us. But if we speed through this time, we risk missing the lessons God wants so much for us to learn. He is such a good and loving teacher, and grief provides many, many opportunities to lean on God and learn from Him. For in grief, we suffer and we need help. So we can turn to Him and discover that He is right there, so very close.

When in a LONG LOW, we can LEAN on God and LISTEN to Him so that we can LEARN the LESSONS He has for us and be LIFTED by His LOVE.

Remember that Christ tells us to:

> Enter by the narrow gate; for wide is the gate and broad is the way that leads to destruction, and there are many who go in by it. Because narrow is the gate and difficult is the way which leads to life, and there are few who find it. (Matthew 7:13–14, NKJV)

The Bible also tells us that:

> Sorrow is better than laughter,
> for sadness has a refining influence on us.
> A wise person thinks a lot about death,
> while a fool thinks only about having a
>   good time.
> (Ecclesiastes 7:3–4, NLT)

Jesus didn't take away my pain by keeping my son from dying at the young age of seventeen. This is a loss that will touch me for the rest of my life. However, because I walk with Jesus, I am not alone and this burden is actually bearable because I am not bearing it on my own. He makes my burden light. Even though I still cry with great sorrow for the son I can no longer hold, the dark valleys filled with tears and sorrow don't last forever. Jesus is there to help me each time I cry; He walks beside me and carries me when I can't walk another step. Eventually, He and I will come to a high mountaintop where I can, again, see the blue sky and the view ahead. He has chosen a new life for me; I have a bright future because I let Jesus lead the way.

A life spent bearing a cross is harder than a life of only happiness and joy. I know that I could have buried a lot of my suffering and grief, and quickly gotten on with my life. If I had, the grief would have returned eventually, making the entire process much more difficult, and I would have missed many important lessons that God had for me to learn. The daily walk of carrying your cross is hard; some days you will have a mountaintop experience and the next you might feel you are in a dark valley. We need to remember that God is with us, no matter what the path is like that day.

> Our walls don't send Him on a pity party. Our wrong choices don't scare Him away. Whatever we're going through right now, He knows. He understands it even more than we do, so we can't think that what we're dealing with might make Him angry at us. He already knows it; He is simply waiting for us to admit it. You see, it is in the admitting that it loses its power over us.
>
> Don't be afraid of making mistakes. Don't worry about runaway emotions. Don't worry about the things that scare you in the deepest parts of your soul—like rejection, like condemnation. Don't be afraid of God. There is nothing in Him to condemn us. He knows, and He loves, and He fights for us more than we could imagine.

> As we rest in Him, He Himself will lead us along the bridal path. After all, He is the only One who knows the way.[17]

Unfortunately, we can be tempted to lose faith along the way and think that God doesn't love us because there are so many trials in our lives. Life is filled with storms and, being human, we will all encounter the fear and doubt that come with these difficult times. When you find yourself staggering in the midst of a storm or trial, reach out to God rather than pulling away from Him. He is the captain of your ship, and He is still in control.

Remember that there are others on this journey alongside you. Through the support and prayers of others, you can find the strength and encouragement you need. Sometimes it is wise to ask for that support. Tell your friends you need prayer. Don't lose faith. Remember that your strongest resource in the midst of suffering is the Lord Himself. Remember consolation versus desolation and say a tiny prayer. Reach out to Him.

One day, we will be able to console and have compassion for others in deep sorrow. For how can we expect to embrace the suffering of others if we can't embrace our own? As Paul says in 2 Corinthians 1:3–5,

> Blessed be the God and Father of our Lord Jesus Christ, the Father of mercies and God of all comfort, who comforts us in all our tribulation, that

---

[17] Jackson, John Paul. *7 Days Behind the Veil: Throne Room Meditations* (Texas, U.S.A.: Streams Publishing House, 2008), p. 32.

we may be able to comfort those who are in any trouble, with the comfort with which we ourselves are comforted by God. For as the sufferings of Christ abound in us, so our consolation also abounds through Christ. (NKJV)

In my journal, I wrote these words:

Lord, today I found that You had made me aware of more tears and grief. My dolly is not here; he is gone from this world, and is there with You. All this is so logical to the outside world, but for me it is hard to sit down in this grief and say the words, "Justin has died."

This grief was brought on by the discovery that my good friend has a benign tumor that is pushing on a nerve in her ear. My thoughts, that I could stand beside her and be a strong comforter, evaporated in this latest wave of grief over my son. Just knowing that my friend is in serious condition has caused the grief to surface again.

And so it does. The waves of grief come again and again, sometimes softly, other times crashing upon the beach of our hearts.

Oftentimes, I don't even realize I need to grieve. But God makes me keenly aware of my grief, if I will only listen to Him. And remembering St. Ignatius' "consolation," I move closer to God and just let the tears fall. A mother's love lives on.

God is our refuge and strength,

A very present help in trouble.

Therefore we will not fear,

Even though the earth be removed,

And though the mountains be carried into the
   midst of the sea;

Though its waters roar and be troubled,

Though the mountains shake with its
   swelling. Selah

There is a river whose streams shall make
   glad the city of God,

The holy place of the tabernacle of the Most
   High.

God is in the midst of her, she shall not be
   moved;

God shall help her, just at the break of dawn.

The nations raged, the kingdoms were
   moved;

He uttered His voice, the earth melted.

The Lord of hosts is with us;

The God of Jacob is our refuge. Selah

Come, behold the works of the Lord,

Who has made desolations in the earth.

He makes wars cease to the end of the earth;

He breaks the bow and cuts the spear in two;

He burns the chariot in the fire.

Be still, and know that I am God;

I will be exalted among the nations,

I will be exalted in the earth!
The Lord of hosts is with us;
The God of Jacob is our refuge. Selah
(Psalm 46:1–11, NKJV)

God has given me all I need. With His help and direction, I can confront my fears and my grief head-on. In turn, I have found healing and the ability to move forward, following His direction for my life and discovering new surprises He has in store for me along the way! I didn't get here overnight, as the path of grieving is long, but by staying close to God I feel I am now turning a corner and can now embrace His plan for me!

I see now what God has done for Justin—He has freed him from the restraints of his wheelchair and the dependence he once had upon others to help him with almost every aspect of his life. When he was with us, Justin would love a day at a mall or any large building where he could just move about freely on smooth floors, but he was still dependent upon us to keep him safe from the dangers of stairs or others who might not notice him. Now Justin is no longer dependent upon his wheelchair or others, and he is free of seizures and the drugs that helped to control them.

Months after writing this statement, and almost two years after Justin died, God caused me to see that I wanted to be in heaven with my son. When he died, I too wanted to die. But God reminded me that I am His bride, and I cannot be a timid bride, but a glorious bride! I must use my gifts to be a servant in His name. It is not yet my time to be in heaven. He is asking me to serve on earth for now, and to accept where He has placed me.

Sometimes we forget that God is the King and we are in His service. We may want to know why the King does certain things, such as taking our loved one at a particular time. But we don't actually need to know the answer. We may be curious, but we will only ever know some of the King's business. In the meantime, we need to continue serving the King. Our hope is in Christ alone, who is our model of a servant. He gives us the Holy Spirit to enable us to serve. It is through Him that we have the power to continue.

A few days later, while visiting with another mother whose special needs son had died only a few months after Justin, God prompted me to buy a large heart-shaped helium balloon which proclaimed, "I love you!" On that balloon, I wrote many other messages with a permanent marker, such as: "I love you, Dolly!" "No more wheelchair!" "No more seizures!" "No more AFOs!" (Justin wore braces on his feet.) "No more medications!" "No more cues—now you can say what you want to say!" And finally, "Mom and Da are glad you are happy and healthy in heaven!" My desire was to release this balloon as a way of renewing my acceptance of where Justin now was and the freedom he now possessed. What I didn't realize was that Dan also needed to be a part of this balloon release. With tears in his eyes, he read the words I had written on the balloon and we made plans to release the balloon together the next day.

We took this balloon to the hill above Justin's school, overlooking the city with the mountains in the distance. As we approached the school, we wondered how we would take a photo of the two of us releasing this balloon, but God had already worked out those details. There on the top of this hill was a young man holding a camera with a long telephoto lens. I walked right up to him, feeling quite sure that God had provided him for such a time as this. He agreed to take some pictures of us releasing our balloon. Little did we know that God had provided someone who specializes in photography! We felt very blessed to have his help on that special day.

God loves us so much! He takes care of the little details. He understands what we are going through and walks with us throughout our journey. Sometimes He holds our hand, and other times He holds us in His hand. But always, He is there.

On Boxing Day, as the second anniversary of Justin's passing approached, I began to experience a very long and steady time of grieving. For two and a half months, I arose each day, ready to get on with my plans, only to discover that my grief was still very much present. Having become accustomed to waves of grief that would come and go, I was surprised by this and was often tempted to think I should be doing more. But God quietly assured me on a daily basis with the words "fine" or "be content"—and with the word "lean." He seemed to be saying that I was doing fine and that all I needed to do was lean on Him.

So that was what I did. I chose to embrace the suffering and listen to God's direction, which often meant laying down my plans for the day. *"For My thoughts are not your thoughts, nor are your ways My ways,' says the Lord"* (Isaiah 55:8, NKJV). I chose to spend more time with God, didn't take on new things, and rested a lot. He would often direct me to go for a walk with our dog rather than do some task I thought was important at the time. And each day He told me to lie down and listen to His words of comfort and direction. Then, after a time, God would direct me to roll over and immediately I fell asleep, tired from the grief and emotion. How important that sleep was, both for my physical and emotional healing.

Friends and family were concerned. Some even worried that I might be depressed. But those closest to me realized that I was still mourning in a healthy way and encouraged me to "stay the course." Mourning is a long process, and everyone grieves differently.

I think we would be wise to ask God what He would have us learn while we are in the crucible of suffering. For it is in these times of trial that we lean the hardest upon Him and can grow the most. Grieving can act as a magnifying glass that draws our attention to those things God wants to point out in our lives. During that long wave of grief, I learned that God is beside me all the way and that I cannot do anything in my own strength; I need Him.

What I Have Gleaned Along the Way

1. Are you really trusting God?

One day, as I struggled with the grief and pain of Justin's passing, God told me, "You do not trust Me." All I knew was that I wanted to be done with God's plan. Oh, how I wanted my son to be here with us again, or to be happily dancing with him in heaven. Yet I knew this was impossible.

Know that you can be honest with God. He loves it when we confide in Him, for honesty is so much healthier than burying our pain.

God doesn't want us to leave the pain and suffering right away; He wants us to embrace our pain first, for it is there in our trials that we must lean on Him and learn from Him. Don't leave. Cleave to the Lord your God. He will strengthen you and uphold you.

God's comfort has continued to be with me as I have struggled with my grief again and again. On occasion, He has given me a special dream, like the one in which I got to have a cuddle from Justin. Many times He has given me a helpful word of encouragement, like the word "happily," reminding me that Justin is now happily running through fields of green on strong legs. God has healed my son; he no longer requires a wheelchair or drugs to help him cope with seizures.

> Trust in the Lord with all your heart
> and lean not on your own understanding;
> in all your ways acknowledge him,
> and he will make your paths straight.
> (Proverbs 3:5–6, NIV)

Trust that He will carry you. Trust that He understands what you need. Trust not in your own understanding and He will make your path straight.

2. "Are you keeping busy?"

Don't rush back to work if you don't have to. While some may have no choice but to work, others work because their pain and grief is so hard to face. Those who return to work prematurely run the risk of delayed grief or denial. This will only cause the wound to resurface at a later time when it will be much harder to deal with.

I would recommend putting off your return to work for several months, or even a year. That might sound extreme, but there is wisdom in it. I could not have known that after six months my grief would still be so strong. If I had been loaded down with responsibilities, my grief might have remained buried, simply because the busyness would have kept me unaware of its existence.

3. Don't run from the grief.

It takes courage to face what the grief holds at each stage of the journey. Don't run away from your feelings or try to hide them. That's not to say that one should get stuck in grief. When the next wave of grief arrives, rather than running from it sometimes it is better to sit down, or literally lie down, and let it wash over you. It is there in our grief that our Lord Jesus speaks. It is in His arms where you will find true healing for your grieving heart.

Don't be afraid to cry. Tears are only water; they can't hurt you. You will likely feel tired afterward. But by listening to your body, and napping if you can, you can move forward without burying your pain.

4. Don't be hard on yourself.

You may not be able to meet every anniversary with glorious joy and celebration, despite your best efforts. Grieving is a long process that will be unique to each individual. It is normal to miss that special person or that special time. Don't feel that you shouldn't grieve; grieving is normal.

5. Don't expect everyone to understand.

Some won't, either because they haven't experienced deep grief yet, or because they have chosen to handle their grief in a different way. Don't contend with them.

You may choose to invite some friends into your pain. It is important to stay close to those friends and family who can support you.

6. Watch out for bitterness.

Some days you may be tempted to become bitter at the people around you because they are not grieving in the same way you are. Remember that everyone grieves differently. We cannot blame someone else for expressing their grief in a different manner. As C.S. Lewis states in his book, *The Horse and His Boy*, "I am telling you your story, not hers. I tell no one any story but his own."[18] We need to worry about our own story.

7. Lay down your expectations.

Avoid burying your grief, as this will likely just delay your grieving process and, in turn, make it more difficult. Secondly, don't have expectations as to how long your grieving process will take. It is best to just let it run its course. Everyone is different. You can be thankful if it lasts a relatively short time. However, you may find that grieving takes much

---

[18] Lewis, C.S. *The Complete Chronicles of Narnia: The Horse and His Boy* (London, U.K.: Harper Collins, 1998), p. 203.

longer than you expected. I was surprised that I encountered a very long period of sorrow at the second anniversary of our son's passing. This wave of grief lasted for two and a half months, and yet God let me know that I was still grieving in a healthy way. He wanted me to be content with the length and breadth of my grieving process and to lean on Him.

I encourage you to hang in there and finish the race. By finishing and not quitting early, you will grow in your relationship with the Lord, you will grow stronger, and you will learn many important lessons along the way. Life is rarely easy, and we often learn our most important lessons through times of trial or suffering. Grief can be a great teacher. As it says in Ecclesiastes 7:3–4, *"Sorrow is better than laughter, for sadness has a refining influence on us"* (NLT).

8. Stay close to Him.

Be careful that you don't leave God behind in your grief. Let Jesus be your guiding light. Let the Holy Spirit speak to you throughout the process, and you won't get lost. It's not what you know, but who you know that makes the difference. *"It is God who arms me with strength and makes my way perfect"* (2 Samuel 22:33, NIV).

9. And finally…

> Be sober, be vigilant; because your adversary the devil walks about like a roaring lion, seeking whom he may devour. Resist him, steadfast in the faith, knowing that the same sufferings are experienced by your brotherhood in the world. But

may the God of all grace, who called us to His eternal glory by Christ Jesus, after you have suffered a while, perfect, establish, strengthen, and settle you. (1 Peter 5:8–10, NKJV)

Psalm 23 says it all. Paraphrased, it reads:

Lord, you have given me the Holy Spirit as
    my shepherd,
Who leads me by the hand to beautiful places,
And beside quiet, peaceful waters.
There I can lay my head down and truly rest
    with You.
Because of You, I have no fears and I do not
    want for anything! You provide all I need.
You restore my soul when I am tired or
    stressed.
You lead me down paths of good, not evil.

Yes, even when I am walking in a time of
    sorrow,
Through a low valley, You are there.
Even when I have been in the presence of
    those who are dying,
I still fear no evil.
You are stronger than my enemy.
Your strength and dependability comfort me
    and give me peace.

You enable me to live and eat in a world,
    surrounded by evil
and my enemies.
You bless me with the oil of blessing;
My life overflows with abundance.
I know You will always provide what is good
    in my life.
You are merciful to me, even though I can
    never earn it.
And I will someday dwell in Heaven with you
    FOREVER!